Eat Up

From left to right: Mark Hix aged 6, Suzi Godson aged 4, Harriet Logan aged 4

Eat Up

Food for children of all ages

Mark Hix

with Suzi Godson

Photographs by Harriet Logan

Consultant Editor: Professor Ian Booth,
Director, Institute of Child Health, University of Birmingham

TED SMART

First published in Great Britain in 2000 by
Fourth Estate Limited
6 Salem Road
London W2 4BU

10 9 8 7 6 5 4 3 2 1

A catalogue record for this book is available from the British Library.

ISBN 1 85613 776 7

Designed by Unlimited
Endpaper illustrations by Scarlet, Ruby and Amber Evans
Pasta illustration page 92 courtesy of Barilla Pasta
Printed in Italy

This edition produced for The Book People Ltd,
Hall Wood Avenue, Haydock, St Helens WA11 9UL

For Ellie, Lydia, Scarlet, Ruby and Amber

Thanks to all the children who turned up to photoshoots. Emily and Max Agace, Esme and Bertie Alexander, Mardi and Otis Azagury Partridge, Anjali Banarjee, Henry and Violet Brand, Alabama Calkin, Megan Calvert, Matilda and Daniel Clarke, Max and Jake Coveney, Lalade and Elizabeth Crystal, Oliver and Isobel Dyson, Rosie Fuest, Shirley Anne Gentry, Zach and Harry Gottlieb, Flora and Kitty Hadaway, Edward Haines, Dunstan Harris, Hector, Owen and Frances Henderson, Nell Hewetson, Katharine and Frances Higgs, William, Rebecca and Jamie Hughes, Charmian and Hirani Innocent, Edie Jones, Edward Jones, Stella Kennedy, Daisy Lawson, Jackson Leighton Logan, Scarlet, Louis and Evie Lingwood, Zsu Zsa Magyar, Antoinette Minella, Alfie Moore, Louis Navayan Courts, Lucy Olley (our cover girl), Kit Pearson, Felix and Madeline Rolt, Jacob Shackleton, Prosper and Romilly Simmons, Frances and Verity Spragge, Millie Stein, Maud and Sidney Thomson, Isobel Veysey, Freddie and Jamie Villiers, Jack and Theo Wilson, Tasnim and Sarah Zarhi.

Many thanks to Liz Allan, Dianne Atkinson, Barilla Pasta, Catherine Blyth, Tony Booth, Scott and Alan at Core Imaging, Mark and Tony Allan at Cutty's, Daisy and Tom, The Early Learning Centre, Ben Evans, Junko Fuwa, Martin Heap at Simply Sausages, Fergus and Margot Henderson, Anthony Hill, Suzie Hix, Patrick Hughes, Justin Leighton, Deborah Logan, St Peters School, Saints, The Shanghai Restaurant, The Singing Tree, Spitalfields Farm, The Spitalfields Organic Co-operative, Charles Spragge, Justine Tabak, and the Taj Stores.

Special thanks must go to mini Boden for generously providing so many beautiful clothes.

Thanks also to Jane Middleton and Professor Ian Booth for reading the text and providing so many helpful insights. Most of all we would like to express our appreciation to Louise Haines, our editor, for her patience, dedication and enthusiasm.

Weights, Measures and Servings

WEIGHT

Metric/Imperial		Metric/Imperial		Metric/Imperial	
7.5g	$1/4$oz	80g	$2\,2/3$oz	330g	11oz
15g	$1/2$oz	90g	3oz	360g	12oz
20g	$3/4$oz	120g	4oz	390g	13oz
30g	1oz	150g	5oz	400g	$13\,1/2$oz
35g	$1\,1/4$oz	180g	6oz	480g	16oz(1lb)
40g	$1\,1/2$oz	210g	7oz	500g	$16\,2/3$oz
50g	$1\,2/3$oz	240g	8oz	720g	$1\,1/2$lb
60g	2oz	250g	$8\,1/3$oz	840g	$1\,3/4$lb
67.5g	$2\,1/4$oz	270g	9oz	960g	2lb
75g	$2\,1/2$oz	300g	10oz	1kg	2lb $1\,1/3$oz

AUSTRALIAN & AMERICAN/EUROPEAN CONVERSIONS

Commodity	USA/Australia	Metric	Imperial
Flour	1 cup	140g	5oz
Caster and granulated sugar	1 cup	225g	8oz
Caster and granulated sugar	2 level tablespoons	30g	1oz
Brown sugar	1 cup	170g	6oz
Butter/margarine/lard	1 cup	225g	8oz
Sultanas/raisins	1 cup	200g	7oz
Currants	1 cup	140g	5oz
Ground almonds	1 cup	110g	4oz
Golden syrup	1 cup	340g	12oz
Uncooked rice	1 cup	200g	7oz
Grated cheese	1 cup	110g	4oz
Butter	1 stick	110g	4oz

OVEN TEMPERATURES

°C	°F	Gas mark	American	Australian
70	150	$1/4$	COOL	VERY SLOW
80	175	$1/4$		
100	200	$1/2$		
110	225	$1/2$		
130	250	1	VERY SLOW	
140	275	1		SLOW
150	300	2	SLOW	
170	325	3	MODERATE	MODERATELY SLOW
180	350	4		
190	375	5	MODERATELY HOT	MODERATE
200	400	6	FAIRLY HOT	
220	425	7	HOT	MODERATELY HOT
230	450	8	VERY HOT	
240	475	8		HOT
250	500	9	EXTREMELY HOT	
270	525	9		VERY HOT
290	550	9		

LIQUID MEASURES

Imperial	ml	fl oz
$1\,3/4$ pints	1000 (1 litre)	35
1 pint	600	20
$1/2$ pint	300	10
$1/4$ pint (1 gill)	150	5
1 teaspoon	5	

AUSTRALIAN

250ml	1 cup
20ml	1 tablespoon
5ml	1 teaspoon

AMERICAN/EUROPEAN CONVERSIONS

American	European
10 pints	4.5 litres/8 pints
$2\,1/2$ pints (5 cups)	1.1 litres/2 pints
1 pint/16 oz	1 pint/20fl oz/600ml
$1\,1/4$ cups	$1/2$ pint/10fl oz/300ml
$1/2$ cup plus 2 tablespoons	$1/4$ pint/5fl oz/150ml
$1/4$ cup	4 tablespoons/2fl oz/55ml
$1/2$ fl oz	1 tablespoon/$1/2$fl oz/15ml
1 teaspoon	1 teaspoon/5ml

Contents

15 To begin with...
25 Shopping
31 Cooking
37 Feeding Babies and Toddlers
39 Weaning Times
41 First Foods
43 Preparing Food for Your Baby
43 The Toddler Years
47 Milk
47 Food Allergies
49 Giorgio Locatelli's Ketchup
49 Salt
49 Food Additives
51 Freezing Children's Foods
51 Freezer Storage Times
51 Equipment

Soups and Stocks

53

57 Vegetable Stock
57 Chicken Stock
59 Carrot and Cumin Soup
59 Tomato Soup
61 Minted Pea Soup
61 Chicken and Sweetcorn Soup
63 Chicken, Vegetable and Lentil Broth
63 Melon Soup
63 Iced Strawberry Soup with Fromage Frais

Vegetables and Salads

67

71 Cumin-roasted Sweet Vegetables
71 Aubergine Escalopes with Melted Mozzarella
73 Caribbean Vegetable Hot-pot
73 Sweet Potato Rösti
75 Proper Mashed Potato
75 Colcannon
77 Chips
77 Parmesan and Rosemary Baked
     Potato Wedges
79 Buttery Sugarsnaps with Smoky Bacon
79 Cumin-spiced Lentils with Coriander
81 Home-made Baked Beans
81 Gratin of Broccoli with Mascarpone
     and Parmesan
83 Little Gems with Thousand Island Dressing
83 Couscous and Herb Salad
85 Greek Salad
85 Crushed Potato Mayonnaise
87 Vegetable Purées
87 Roast Pumpkin and Ginger Purée
89 Pea Purée
89 Celeriac and Apple Mash
91 Bashed Neeps
91 Tim's Carrot Purée with Basil

Eggs, Pasta and Rice

95

99 Spanish Tortilla
99 Coddled Eggs
101 Scrambled Eggs with Chicken Livers
101 Pasta Pomodoro
103 Pasta e Fagioli
103 Penne with Tuna, Tomato and Olive Oil
105 Farfalle with Pesto
105 Giant Pasta Shells with Chicken and Herbs
107 Butternut Squash Risotto
107 Potato Gnocchi
109 Spinach, Leek and Parmesan Risotto
109 Spring Herb Risotto with Courgettes

👍 Indicates the recipes that are suitable for younger babies

113 Meat and Fish

117 Granny's Home-cooked Ham
117 Lamb's Liver with Bacon, Mash
     and Savoy Cabbage
119 Bangers and Mash with Onion Gravy
119 Toad in the Hole
121 Shepherd's Pie
123 Little Chicken and Ham Pies
125 Roast Poussin with Bread Sauce
127 Coronation Chicken
127 Parmesan-fried Chicken Escalopes
129 Fergus Henderson's Crispy Pig's Tails
131 Hamburgers
131 Paul Heathcote's Lancashire Hot-pot
135 Smoked Haddock with Poached Egg
     and Colcannon
135 Cod Fillet with Parsley Sauce and Mash
137 Real Fish Fingers
137 Salmon Casserole with Petits Pois
139 Kedgeree
139 Fishcakes with Herb Sauce
141 Tuna Burgers
141 Tuna Bolognese Sauce
143 Fish Pie with Fennel

147 Puddings

149 Chocolate Chip Cookies
151 Creamy Sweet Polenta with Mango
     and Mascarpone
151 Sophie's Apricot and Vanilla Compote
153 Sweet Couscous with Raisins and Yoghurt
153 Rhubarb Cream
155 Simple Little Chocolate Pots
155 Henry Harris's Meringues, Cranberries
     and Ice Cream
157 Pancakes
157 Raspberry and Peach Crumble
159 Elderflower Jelly with Summer Fruits
159 Jam Roly Poly
161 Pain Perdu with Roasted Banana
161 Blueberry Muffins
163 Summer Fruit and Amaretti Cake
165 Chocolate and Pineapple Sticks
165 Tropical Fruit Salad with Star Anise
167 Eton Mess with Strawberries
167 Jeremy Strode's Coconut Sorbet

171 Picnics, Snacks and Parties

175 Koftas with Minted Yoghurt
175 Courgette and Parmesan Sticks
177 Waffles
177 Tomato and Polenta Fingers
179 Scotch Quail's Eggs
179 Corn Fritters
181 Crudités with Guacamole
181 Houmous
183 Thai Summer Rolls
183 Sweet Potato and Parsnip Crisps
185 Chicken Satay with Peanut Sauce
187 Tortillas
187 Croque Enfant
189 Chocolate Toasties
189 Eggy Bread
191 Double Chocolate Rice Pyramid

195 Drinks and Lollies

197 Lemonade
197 Pear and Ginger Juice
199 Strawberry and Banana Smoothie
199 Banana Smoothie
199 Banana and Peanut Butter Smoothie
199 Tropical Fruit Smoothie
201 Vanilla Milkshake
201 Banana Fromage Frais Milkshake
201 Lollipops

204 Index

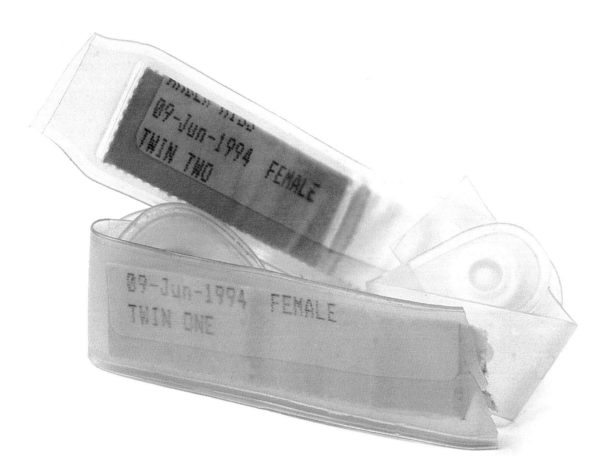

To begin with...

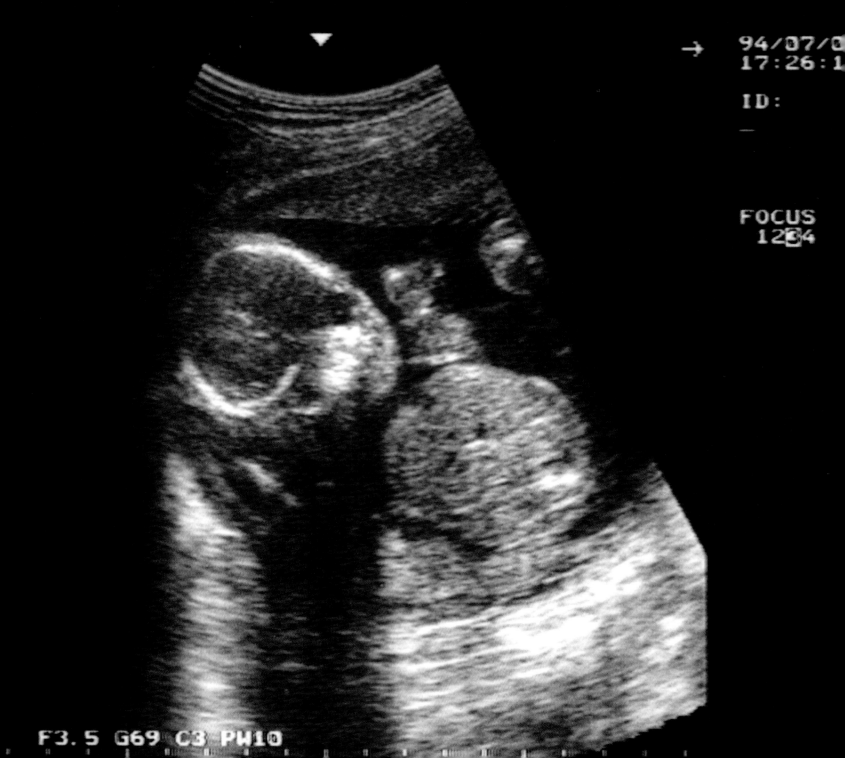

When our twin girls, Ellie and Lydia, were born, like many fathers I didn't feel I could get very involved in feeding them. Initially, they were breastfed but this was exhausting for my wife, Suzie, so we were both relieved when they started drinking formula milk because it meant we could share the almost constant feeding. A diet consisting entirely of formula seemed an awful way for babies to inaugurate their tastebuds but mine drank pints of the stuff and the fridge was crammed with 8oz bottles for months. I couldn't wait to get them on to proper food.

When they finally moved on to 'solids', I sampled a few jars of baby food out of curiosity. Although they're supposed to be completely natural I didn't think they tasted anything like their original ingredients. As a chef, I had ambitions for Ellie's and Lydia's little palates even then, and I would experiment with purées of freshly cooked vegetables at the weekends and freeze them for Suzie to use during the week. My schedule was so hectic that getting to feed Ellie and Lydia, or even eating together as a family, was a rare treat, so I concentrated on making their food a bit special. We wanted to get them used to flavour and variety but, even more importantly, by making their food at home we knew exactly what was in it. Commercially processed food can be a valuable standby but it is not nearly as tasty as the fresh, home-cooked alternative.

In a professional kitchen, chefs create dishes by mixing complementary flavours, whether it's carrot and cardamom, beetroot and horseradish or something as classic as peas and mint. With Ellie and Lydia we used potato and parsnip as a base to introduce vegetables such as pumpkin, carrots, leeks and other root vegetables. As they got older, we added small quantities of spices such as cumin and fresh ginger. We put everything we could in the blender and sometimes the purées were so tasty that Suzie and I would eat a chunkier version as an accompaniment to meat or fish.

It became apparent early on that Ellie and Lydia preferred the taste of banana and sweet vegetables such as parsnip and butternut squash to more savoury flavours such as avocado and potato. What I found interesting about the purée stage was the fact that, because all the food has the same smooth consistency, likes and dislikes are based entirely on taste, not appearance, texture or presentation. It was much easier feeding Ellie and Lydia at this stage. Their senses of smell and taste were pure and they were happy to explore new flavours in a way that they would later become much more reluctant to do. After the first few months texture and presentation become increasingly important.

Although presentation is not important to a small baby, variety is. If babies are given the same pale purée at every meal, the chances are that when they are eventually offered carrot or avocado they will be less willing to try it. Habits are formed very early, so offering different colours and flavours at the beginning helps keep lots of options open. Feeding children is very different from feeding adults. Feeding a small baby is about anticipating and satisfying a physical need, whereas the adults that I feed in restaurants are not necessarily hungry at all. Adults appreciate that food is a pleasure and that taste is a sensory experience. Whether they are hungry or not, having dinner at the Ivy is an enjoyable thing to do. With Ellie and Lydia, however, I learned the hard way that, unless they were hungry, the effort of producing a meal for them was wasted, no matter how good the food was. Timing is crucial in a restaurant but it is even more important with a small baby.

From about seven months, the girls began to learn how to feed themselves, and mealtimes became very messy. We were never sure how much food they actually swallowed because most of it seemed to end up on the floor, but they were healthy and growing so we didn't worry. Things became more interesting the older they got. By the time they were tucking into finger foods,

like pieces of bread and fruit, and enjoying soft-textured dishes such as risotto, mashed vegetables, fish pie and shepherd's pie, there was very little difference between what they liked and what we liked. I've always been quite partial to nursery food, so cooking separate meals for them seemed unnecessary. I would cook a simple butternut squash risotto for the girls, and finish it off with butter, salt and pepper for Suzie and myself. It seemed like common sense to cook for the whole family at once rather than cater for two separate meals – I had to cook a 'second sitting' at the restaurant and I certainly didn't intend to start doing it at home as well.

However, as Ellie and Lydia became more independent, feeding them became less straightforward. By the time they were toddlers they had worked out that mealtimes were an opportunity to assert themselves. In retrospect I suppose Suzie and I made all the obvious mistakes. We really wanted them to eat and they soon cottoned on to the fact that if they refused to eat something they would eventually be offered an alternative. Because there were two of them, despite our best intentions their combined demands would send us running to the fridge to try and find something more acceptable, when in fact if they had been hungry they would probably have eaten the first dish anyway. Snacking was part of the problem. Toddlers use up a lot of energy but if they are given 'something to keep them going' often enough they won't be able to eat a proper meal. So we tried to exert a bit of 'snack control' to ensure the twins were hungry at mealtimes. If they then rejected something it was likely to be because they genuinely disliked it rather than because they were being fussy or just weren't hungry.

For many parents, problems can arise as soon as their children have their first taste of convenience foods. The simple answer, of course, is to steer well clear of them but nowadays there is such a strong assumption that children should eat special 'children's foods' (despite the fact that these are often packed with sugar and additives) that they can be difficult to resist. Children are frequently offered these foods outside the home anyway and they usually love them.

So gradually 'child-friendly' processed, prepacked, flavour-enhanced convenience foods, loaded with additives and preservatives, creep into the fridge. Now there is very little wrong with an occasional meal of fish fingers, boiled potatoes, peas and ketchup but if any food appears too frequently in a child's diet it is at the expense of another. The child becomes wary of other types of food and getting them to eat a varied diet becomes difficult.

It is so much easier to persuade children to accept new flavours and foods if they are given a wide experience of new textures and tastes in their first year and are never given the option of eating rubbish in the first place. I know it is virtually impossible to keep them away from junk food indefinitely, but in the home at least you can make a rule that there is only good, unprocessed food on offer. If kids are hungry enough they will eat anything, but when they are given the choice between an apple and a packet of sweets, the sweets win every time. The best solution is to offer them a choice between an apple and a banana instead.

The range of foods children are offered is significant. If they are offered only ten different types of food, you can be pretty sure that they will refuse three and moan about two. If they are offered 50 types of food, even if they refuse 25 they are still eating a decent variety and will be getting a better nutritional balance.

Manufacturers have successfully exploited the significant role that packaging plays in determining whether a food product gets into the shopping trolley or not. Yoghurts are an extreme example. Once considered to be healthy, they are now just an extension of the sweetie counter, with lots of sugar, chemical additives, and cartons that feature children's favourite television characters. Even apples come wrapped in Mister Men packaging. Trying to get around the supermarket with small children is a nightmare if you don't want to end up with a trolley full of junk. When I am shopping with Ellie and Lydia I usually give them a bag of grapes to chomp on, which lasts until we get past the rubbish through to the fresh bread. Then I get a baguette and they break the ends off and chew on those. On a good day, this plan will get me to the checkout without any whingeing.

Because food plays such an important part in my life, I am probably more pushy than most when it comes to what my children eat but I do realise that there's no point having unrealistic expectations. Like most children their age, Ellie and Lydia have very strong likes and dislikes, and just because I want them to acquire a taste for a particular food doesn't mean they will. I never force them to eat anything because it would probably be counterproductive but I do insist that they try something before they tell me they don't like it. Letting them take charge in the kitchen is a good way of getting them to try foods they might otherwise reject. Neither Ellie nor Lydia used to like eggs very much until I got them to help me make coddled eggs. They stood on chairs to crack the eggs into little pots, then watched them cook in the oven, and were keen to eat them when they were ready. I like to let them help me squeeze fresh orange juice, too, so they see how much mess and effort is involved in producing a small amount. Because there isn't much

they savour it, and when we compare it to the processed taste of orange squash they can see how far removed the real thing is from its commercial cousin.

If there is only a tiny amount of something available it tends to seem much more desirable to them, so serving very small portions of any food that has taken time to prepare is a good tactic. Adults often forget that a small child's stomach is only the size of their clenched fist, so they can't eat very big portions. It is better to serve them less and let them ask for more than to load their plate.

When I want Ellie and Lydia to taste something unusual I tend not to offer it to them at mealtimes. Instead I make a distinction between 'tasting' and 'eating', with tasting as a no-pressure opportunity to explore flavour. Some children enjoy doing a blindfold quiz, where they have to guess what they are eating and say whether they like it. It's easiest to start with teaspoons of flavoured liquids – anything from elderflower to Marmite. Sometimes we do food comparisons, when, for example, I buy three types of tomato and get the twins to help me choose which one tastes best.

When Ellie and Lydia developed a passion for 'anything with breadcrumbs' and started to take an unhealthy interest in junk food, I decided the best way to steer them back on to decent food was to imitate the things they liked but to cook them myself, using good fresh ingredients. Hamburgers make a very nutritious meal if they are prepared from good-quality minced beef. Fishfingers made with fresh cod or haddock fillet and coated in freshly prepared breadcrumbs are a great alternative to the shopbought versions, and even thick-cut chips or potato wedges made at home contain lots of nutrients and less fat than the frozen variety. Although I realise this is hardly pushing the frontiers of flavour, at least Ellie and Lydia now know what real minced beef or fish tastes like. I have also persevered in trying to find ways of including ingredients they don't like in their diet, so now, though they won't eat leeks, for example, they love leek and potato soup.

Eating out regularly can help to stimulate children's interest in food. Many parents are put off by the fear that their children will create an embarrassing noise and mess, but if kids are introduced to eating out early on they soon adapt to the different environment. Though they are only four, I regularly take Ellie and Lydia to Chinatown in London for *dim sum* or to Brick Lane for Indian food. Ethnic restaurants tend to have a friendlier, less stuffy approach to children, which means that everyone can relax. We order lots of small dishes and, though the girls certainly won't eat everything, they don't feel under any pressure so they tend to be more adventurous than usual. Eating 'tapas style' allows kids to experience a wide variety of different flavours at the same time and this is not something that can be easily recreated at home.

Another advantage of ethnic restaurants is that children are expected to eat the same food as adults. Going to a restaurant and ordering proper food for yourself and a 'children's menu' of cheap sausages and chips for the kids totally defeats the purpose of taking them to a restaurant in the first place. Separating children's food from adults' can only add to the problem if you are trying to educate them to eat properly. For so many small children, dinner is something served in a plastic bowl at 6pm while their parents try and get on with something else. It's no wonder that they fail to see it as an enjoyable social occasion. It is difficult for many families to eat together during the week because of early bedtimes and long working hours but at least we can try and redress the balance at weekends.

I believe that children do prefer to eat good food but a lot of them just don't get the opportunity. Providing home-cooked meals for them is one way of making sure that they do. Cooking fresh ingredients is more labour-intensive than relying on convenience food but it is also more nutritious, more satisfying and less expensive (think of the price of a carrot compared to the price of a jar of carrot purée). The long-term gain is that the whole family becomes healthier and more adventurous in its tastes.

The recipes in this book are basically classic dishes or adaptations that I feel would be suitable for adults and children to enjoy together. On the whole they are very simple to make, because there's no point spending an inordinate amount of time cooking something that your two-year-old might hate. Because children have such different tastes, they won't like all the recipes, but persevere and they may well surprise you. When we took the kids to the London restaurant, St John, to meet Fergus Henderson, who had cooked up a big plate of pig's tails, I could never have guessed that Ellie and Lydia would tuck in with such gusto.

I hope this book will encourage parents to make fresh food for their children. Sure, you can go out and buy a bottle of lemonade but making it yourself is easy, infinitely healthier and tastes of what it is supposed to taste of – fresh lemons. That's really what this book is all about.

Shopping

Because I love food I actually enjoy shopping, though I am the first to confess that I am not usually pushing a trolley full of nappies and cornflakes. I like to go to Covent Garden market every Tuesday morning at 5am to find out what's available. Interestingly, I have only ever bumped into one other chef there, though if you believe the press the place should be crawling with them. Many chefs rely on their suppliers to bring new foods to them but I find that wandering around myself keeps me in touch and also gives me fresh ideas about what to cook. If I invite people to dinner, they are often surprised when they ask me what I am cooking and I say that I don't know because I haven't been shopping yet. But if I try and plan dishes in advance I often can't find one of the key ingredients anyway, so I like to keep an open mind. If I find a good main ingredient I can usually match the rest of the meal around it with what's available. In the same way, I quite often find myself creating dishes with what's left in my fridge at home. Lots of well-known dishes have been invented in this way – for example, Caesar salad. Who would ever think of matching anchovies, Parmesan, garlic, romaine lettuce and croutons? That's what Caesar Cardini did when guests turned up at his hotel unexpectedly and he had nothing to feed them.

Though supermarkets nowadays are ahead of the game, unfortunately they are often ahead of the seasons, too. I find it sad that, just as we are all becoming more sophisticated about food, our awareness of the seasons is being destroyed. Supermarkets aim to supply everything all the time, regardless of where it comes from, what the season is, whether it is ripe, and, most important of all, whether it has any flavour. Yes, in theory, it's great to be able to cook with anything you like all year round, but what's the point if it doesn't taste of much? Certain foods are only worth eating in season, such as tomatoes and berries. As a child, I used to look forward to the appearance of my grandfather's first strawberries in June, but now that we can eat imported ones all year round – greenhouse-grown and tasteless – the magic has gone. So although I envy kids today the huge variety of food they can pick and choose from, at the same time I worry that everything is beginning to taste like everything else – is it any wonder they get bored?

I want to keep alive for my children the tastes and scents of the food that I enjoyed as a child and I believe the best way to do this is to buy seasonally. When it comes to organic food, I have yet to be convinced that it always tastes better. Some organic produce has a superb flavour – chicken, eggs and carrots are obvious examples – but too much of what's available consists of disappointing and expensive foreign imports. The best way to buy organic is to subscribe to a box scheme, where organic produce is delivered to your door. In this way you can be sure that what you're getting is fresh and locally produced, and prices will be more reasonable because you are buying direct from the producer. Farmers' markets can be good sources of organic food, too.

In terms of health, organic food is undoubtedly a better choice for children, since it is grown without the use of pesticides, and animals are raised without routine antibiotics and growth promoters. Although 'safe' levels of toxins have been established (but not always adhered to), these are based on adult intake. Children have less body mass and so consume a proportionally higher amount – particularly babies, for whom fruit and vegetables are a major source of nutrition. At the same time, their immature immune systems are less able to cope with toxins in their diet. As a parent I worry about the potential effect on my children's health of modern farming methods but I'm also concerned about the lack of diversity. Supermarket demands for uniform produce with a long shelf life have resulted in the loss of hundreds of varieties of fruits and vegetables. The quest for cheap meat has led to the loss of traditional breeds and an intensive farming system that has become tainted by disease – even eggs are no longer considered a safe food for our children. Supermarkets now package food with 'grown for flavour' on the labels because so much produce tastes of nothing. Surely beyond 'eating to live', the whole point of food is flavour, and the best way to achieve this is to go back to more natural farming methods.

Cooking

At school, when it came to the crunch at the end of the fifth form, I was completely clueless about what to do with my life. All my mates became golf pros and if I had been serious enough about it I could have followed them. I had a seven handicap by the time I was 15 and played three times every weekend and as often as I could during the week.

In our last year at school we had to choose between metalwork and domestic science. I couldn't see the point in filing away at a bit of metal for weeks to end up with a key ring, so I opted for cooking. I was teased a lot, but once I got into making pineapple upside-down cake I started to enjoy it. When I beat all the girls and won the school domestic science prize, the careers officer suggested that I apply to catering college. I never imagined that making that small decision would turn into my big career opportunity but once I got to college I never looked back.

My lecturer at Weymouth College, Laurie Mills, became an inspiration. We hit it off immediately and his passion for food was contagious. He had worked at the Dorchester and Grosvenor House hotels in London, where I was later to follow in his footsteps. His approach was very relaxed and he taught me that cooking for a living was not only great fun but also socially acceptable.

My style of cooking still reflects the things I learned when I was growing up, and it's a style that works well at home, too. I use the best seasonal ingredients I can find and stick to natural combinations of flavours. Maybe snacking on my friend Mark Hawker's dad's queen scallops in the school playground taught me this lesson at an early age. I don't believe in fussy, complicated techniques or presentation, and the older I get the less I try to create new combinations. The main ingredient should always be good enough to speak for itself. If you find a really great piece of fish, why try and complicate the dish and end up masking its flavour?

When I was training to be a chef we studied classic French cooking because the French seemed to own cuisine in a way that we British never could. French cooking was difficult, intimidating and sophisticated. Cookery books were all the same – everything came with tricky sauces or had to be braised with a hundred different flavourings. We learned the French term for every single ingredient, and even now, when I eat out in France, I can order in immaculate French but I can't ask for directions to the loo. Though some people still believe that proper cooking involves complicated sauces and pyrotechnics, I find that most of the best dishes I come up with have no more than three complementary main ingredients, and I like to be able to taste all of them.

This doesn't mean that I always play safe when I'm cooking. I enjoy creating dishes and I've got to the stage where I don't need to worry too much about culinary correctness because, after years as a chef, I have developed a reasonable understanding of what works and what doesn't. This is the key to good cooking, yet there's no mystery about it. If you like food and you are keen to learn, you can do the same. Just keep practising and always be open to ideas – magazines, books, television and restaurants are all excellent sources of inspiration and will help you refine your culinary sensibilities.

If you want to cook for your children but lack confidence in the kitchen, remember that preparing food for a small child is a great way of developing an understanding of ingredients and flavour. It's fascinating to witness small children trying foods for the first time and it can help you to rethink tastes you've taken for granted for years – all those simple purées, for example, reveal how sweet many vegetables are and how surprisingly acidic fruit can be.

Don't make the mistake of thinking that flavour is unimportant to small children. Given a choice between boiled vegetables or the significantly more tasty vegetables roasted with herbs and olive oil, most adults would automatically choose the latter –

and, not surprisingly, most children would, too. As soon as they are old enough (around eight months) you can begin to add small quantities of flavourings such as herbs, ginger and garlic to their food. If, like me, you prefer to keep things simple when cooking, you will find that flavour is determined largely by the quality of the ingredients you use (unless, of course, you cremate them during cooking). You don't need to overdo flavours, especially when cooking for children – just trust the ingredients to do their work. Even the subtle flavour of the oil a food is cooked in will add to the taste of the final dish – particularly with Italian food, which is one of the best examples of culinary simplicity and also one of the most appealing cuisines for children.

Nowadays no one needs to cook in order to survive but there's so much more pleasure to be had from cooking than from choosing a packet out of the chill cabinet of the supermarket. And if your children grow up surrounded by the sights and smells of cooking – a soup simmering on top of the stove, a roast chicken being taken from the oven, fruit being puréed to make a smoothie – they are far more likely to appreciate good food and the effort that goes into making it.

Feeding Babies and Toddlers

Weaning Times

The chart below indicates when you can safely introduce foods to your baby's diet. With the notable exceptions of whole milk, gluten and nuts, from a nutritional point of view most foods are appropriate for children once they have been weaned. It is really a question of texture – if it's not smooth or small enough for your child to swallow, do not give them it.

From 4 months:
Baby rice
Carrot
Potato
Parsnip
Swede
Courgette
Cauliflower
Green beans
Sweet potato
Banana
Apple
Pear
Papaya
Pumpkin and squash
  (such as butternut squash)
Broccoli
Tomato
Spinach
Peas
Celery
Leek
Sweet peppers
Avocado
Melon
Plum
Apricot
Peach
Kiwi fruit
Soft dried fruit

From 6 months:
Foods containing gluten
  (e.g. bread, pasta, wheat
  and oat cereals)
Cheese
Butter
Yoghurt
Full-fat milk (in cooking only
  not as a drink)
Chicken
Meat
Sweetcorn
Citrus fruit
Berries (e.g. strawberries,
  raspberries, blueberries)
Mango

From 8–9 months:
Fish (except shellfish)
Well-cooked eggs
Beans and pulses
Smooth peanut butter and
  other nut butters (as long
  as there is no family history
  of nut or seed allergies, in
  which case delay until after
  3 years)

From 1 year:
Full-fat milk to drink
  (or a formula is better.
  See page 47.)

From 2 years:
Shellfish

From 5 years:
Whole nuts and seeds

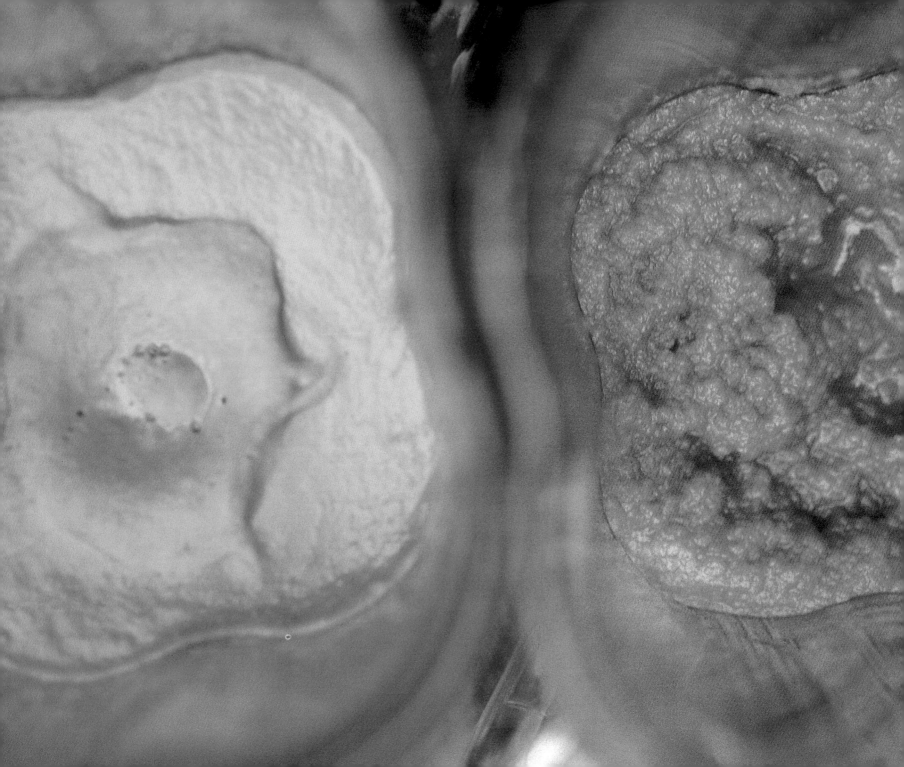

First Foods

Until babies are four months old, their digestive system is not ready to cope with anything except milk and they don't have the necessary muscle control to swallow solid food. From four months, they begin to let their parents know that they are ready for solids. If your baby is drinking a lot of milk but still seems hungry all the time, it is probably time to introduce a little baby rice at one feed. This is similar in taste to the milk your baby is used to, and is rich in iron and vitamins.

Baby rice is a single-grain cereal, which means that if your baby has an allergic reaction to it you will know that rice is the cause. If you begin with a mixed-grain cereal, or a fruit and rice cereal, you won't be able to identify which element has triggered a reaction. Mix the baby rice to a semi-liquid consistency with breast milk, formula milk or cooled boiled water. One teaspoon of rice mixed with three teaspoons of liquid should be enough to begin with. Many parents don't get through a single box of baby rice before their babies are on to more exciting flavours, so don't stock up on too much of it.

Once your baby is familiar with rice, it is time to introduce the more interesting flavours of vegetable and fruit purées. Because babies naturally like sweet things anyway, it is a good idea to start them off on the savoury taste of vegetable purées, and save fruit until a bit later. Purées made from fresh ingredients have a stronger, more distinctive flavour than commercial baby food and, if they are properly cooked, contain nutrients that are frequently lost in processing. I find the one exception to fresh vegetables is the humble pea, which is better cooked from frozen. Home-made purées are much cheaper than jars of food, and you can make a batch in advance and then freeze it in tiny portions in ice-cube trays. The cubes can then be thawed in minutes when you need them.

It is best to treat the introduction of solids as a fun experiment initially. Be prepared for lots of mess and don't expect your baby to eat very much. These early tastes are more about education than nutrition. Your baby should continue to drink the same amount of milk, which will still be the main source of nourishment.

It is not a good idea to give babies their first taste of solids when they are hungry. They don't know what is happening when they feel a spoon being put into their mouth, since they are used to a continuous flow of milk and have no idea how to use their mouths to eat in a different way. Making them learn this when they are anxious to be fed is a recipe for disaster, so take the edge off their hunger by giving them their usual milk first.

Use a tiny shallow plastic spoon which will be soft on your baby's gums and don't put it too far into the mouth. Babies know how to suck and swallow, so if you place the spoon to their lips they can suck the food into their mouth, taste it and swallow it.

Don't force your baby to eat. If they are not hungry or just not ready for solids, they won't respond. Take no for an answer and leave it at that. If eating starts out as a difficult experience, it may stay that way. However, if you introduce a new food and your baby does not like the taste, don't give up on it entirely. Try it again a week or so later and you may well get a much more enthusiastic response. Something else they do like eating is probably providing any missing nutrients especially if your baby is still drinking breastmilk or formula. As long as your baby is healthy, happy and growing, you can safely assume that all is well.

Babies' body language tells us a lot about how hungry they are and whether they like something. When babies are hungry they appear excited by waving their hands, kicking their feet and leaning forward to open their mouths. If they are not hungry they close their mouths and turn their heads away, or fall asleep.

Babies lose more water than adults and need to be kept well hydrated, especially if they are ill. Don't be tempted to give them sugary drinks. It will encourage a taste for sweet things that might make them difficult to feed later on and if they have any teeth the sugar could damage them. Milk, plus water from the age of about eight months, is all they need.

Preparing Food for Your Baby

The consistency of the food you give your baby is important. At first they should have very smooth, semi-liquid purées. To make these, cook vegetables or fruit until very soft, then purée in a blender and strain through a sieve. Dilute with a little cooled boiled water if necessary. From six to seven months you can introduce foods with a little more texture – potatoes, for example, can be mashed rather than puréed. Check that there are no large lumps by running a fork through before serving. Babies can't chew or spit things out, so if they find a big lump in their mouth they will try and swallow it, and may choke. As they grow, textured foods allow a baby to develop chewing skills in anticipation of the arrival of teeth.

For the first couple of months you should sterilise all the bowls, spoons and cups you use for feeding your baby, and after that be scrupulously hygienic when preparing food. Food for babies should always be properly cooked and then allowed to cool before serving. Don't reheat any food and, if your baby doesn't finish something, throw it away. If you are warming food in a microwave you need to make sure it is evenly heated. Microwaves cook from the inside out, so the surface may be the right temperature while the inside is boiling hot. Always stir well and taste it yourself before giving it to your child. Food stays warmer for longer in plastic and cools quicker in china.

At about eight or nine months old, your baby will be trying finger foods such as crusty bread, pieces of banana, soft fruits such as peaches, and lightly cooked vegetable sticks. Although they are very keen to feed themselves at this stage, they are not very experienced, so you need to keep an eye on them to make sure they don't choke. Poking, smearing and squidging food helps them to learn about it. Not much gets into their mouth but the process of exploration is important. You don't need to worry too much about a balanced diet at this stage as their nutritional needs are still being met by milk. The more food they eat, the less milk they will need, but they should still have a high fluid intake. Introducing drinks of cooled boiled water will keep them hydrated without interfering with their appetite.

The Toddler Years

As your baby gets older it should be enjoying a wide variety of tastes and textures, and its mealtimes should gradually fall in line with your own. Once your baby can eat pretty much everything that you can (at about 12 months), it's time to start cooking for everyone at the same time and just mashing or puréeing food for your baby where appropriate.

Feeding toddlers can become more difficult as they start asserting their independence. They quickly realise that one of the easiest ways to do this is to refuse the food that their anxious parents are trying to persuade them to eat. Most parents worry at some stage that their child is not eating enough, and it's tempting to compromise by giving in to demands for snacks or sweet foods instead of proper meals. At this critical time, it is important to stick to your principles and continue to offer healthy food at regular intervals.

No child will intentionally starve itself but a child that is constantly offered alternative dishes will soon exploit this situation for all it's worth. And, of course, some of them just lose interest in food. This is where presentation becomes important. Food on sticks like koftas or satay is fun to eat, and dipping foods such as crudités with guacamole are messy but very nutritious. Eating together as a family and allowing your toddler to dip in and take bits and pieces of your meal is the best way of getting them to enjoy the whole sociable experience of eating without putting them under too much pressure.

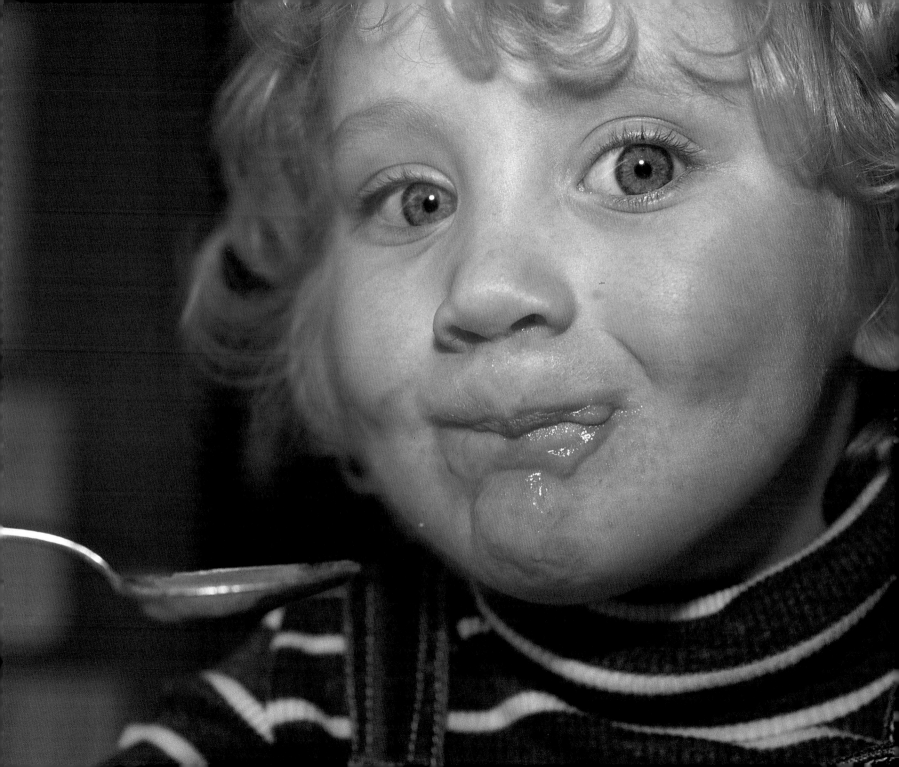

Milk

From about seven months you can start using whole cow's milk in your cooking. You should continue breastfeeding or feeding your baby formula feed until 12 months. Making the switch to full-fat milk as a drink should happen at about one year, though your baby can eat dairy produce such as yoghurt and cheese from about six months. The use of unmodified (pasteurised) cow's milk as a drink should be avoided before 12 months because it is a very poor source of iron, and is low on vitamins, particularly those essential vitamins C and D. Alternatively, a so-called 'follow-on formula' can be used, although the benefits over an ordinary formula are not well defined.

If your baby is reluctant to take solids which are rich in iron (red meats and green vegetables) it is wise to continue a milk formula to 18 months. Don't give skimmed or semi-skimmed milk to babies and children under five as they need the calories and fatty acids that full-fat milk provides. We are so used to the idea that a healthy diet is a low-calorie one that it's easy to forget that small children need calories to help them grow.

Very occasionally babies suffer from a condition called lactose intolerance, which means that they lack an enzyme in the intestine required to break down the sugar in milk into simpler sugars. If you suspect your baby might be lactose intolerant (symptoms include nausea, bloating, wind and diarrhoea) you should seek advice from your GP.

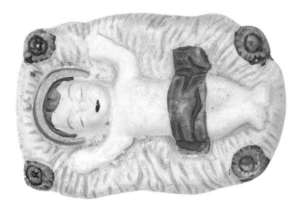

Food Allergies

Allergic reactions to foods are uncommon in infancy and probably affect less than 2% of babies. Vomiting, diarrhoea, skin rashes and poor weight gain are the usual symptoms and cow's milk is the usual culprit. The reactions occur after each exposure to the food, and a single vomit or loose stool should not be interpreted as a sign of food allergy. Other foods which most frequently cause allergic reactions in this age group are eggs, soya, wheat, citrus fruit, fish and peanuts. In rare cases, the reaction can be severe, and cause the rapid onset of swelling of the lips and face, and breathing difficulties (anaphylaxis). If this happens dial 999.

Children almost always grow out of the food allergies they experience as babies, but it may take two to three years. It is therefore wise to seek medical advice if you think your baby is showing an allergic reaction to a food. In particular, it is important to make sure that by excluding an offending food you are not giving your baby a nutritionally inadequate diet (by excluding milk for example). It is also wise to reintroduce the food under medical supervision.

Food allergies are much more likely to happen if there is a history of allergies in your family, in which case you can minimise the risks of food allergy by breastfeeding for as long as possible. Don't introduce solids until four to six months of age and start with foods that are least likely to cause allergic reactions, such as single-grain cereals, vegetables and non-citrus fruits. If you buy processed food always read the label.

Try not to worry when introducing new foods to your child – remember that food allergies affect only a tiny minority. If your child does develop allergies, my fellow chef Giorgio Locatelli is a shining example of how to cope with them. When his daughter, Marguerita, was one year old it turned out she was allergic to a whole host of different foods. This put poor Marguerita in hospital, where she had all sorts of tests. Giorgio has to exercise all his culinary skills when cooking for her and he has invented a remarkable ketchup recipe. In case you are ever unfortunate enough to find yourself in a similar situation, here it is.

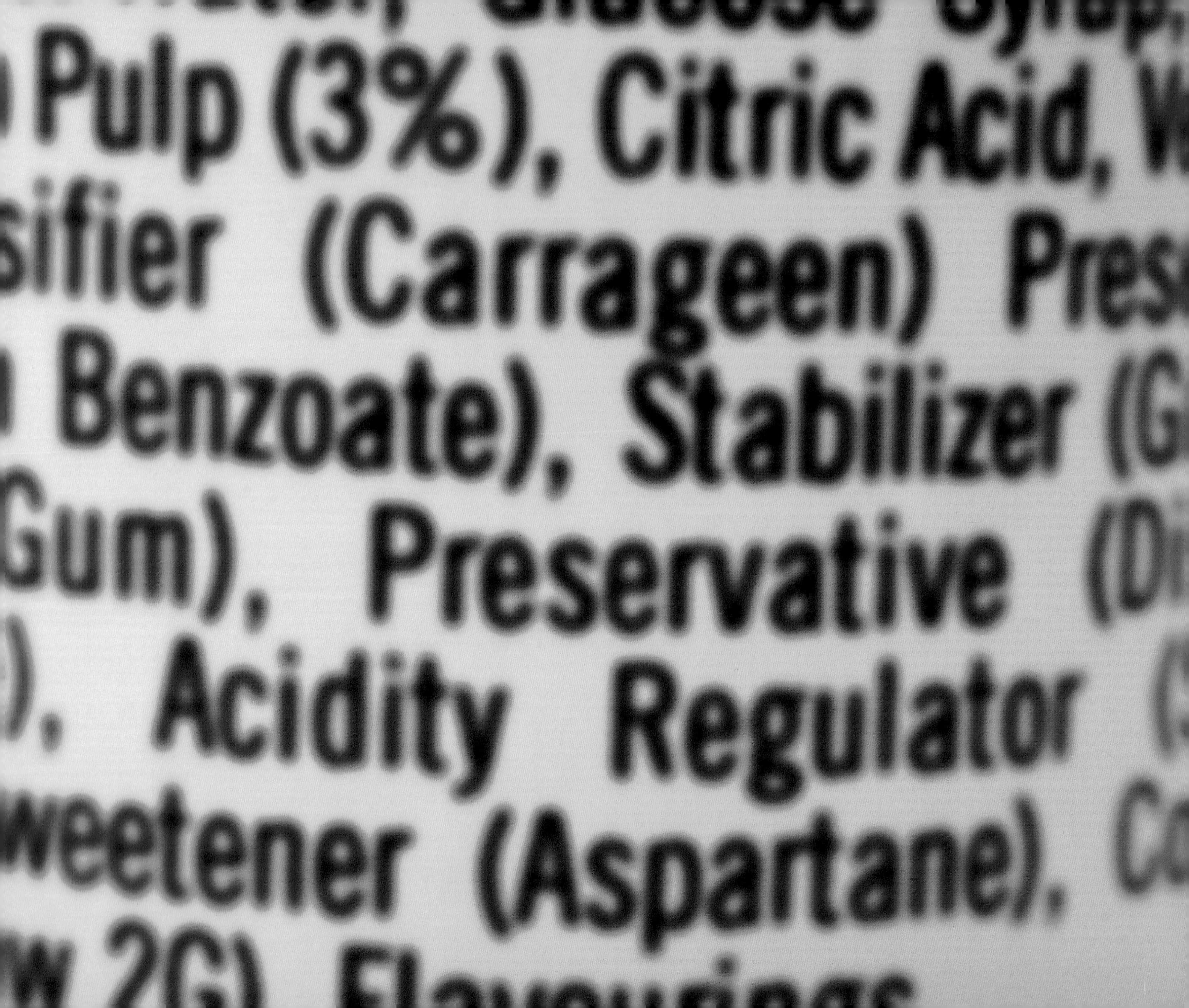

Pulp (3%), Citric Acid, W
sifier (Carrageen) Pres
Benzoate), Stabilizer (G
Gum), Preservative (Di
), Acidity Regulator (
weetener (Aspartane). C
w 2G) Flavourings

Giorgio Locatelli's Ketchup

2 tablespoons olive oil
3 onions, peeled and finely chopped
2 cloves of garlic, peeled and crushed
3 tablespoons water
2 ripe bananas, peeled and chopped
1 tablespoon soy sauce
2 teaspoons brown sugar
2 tablespoons white wine vinegar
Juice of 1/2 lemon

Heat the olive oil in a saucepan and gently cook the onion until soft. Add the garlic and continue to cook for a couple of minutes. Add all the remaining ingredients, bring to the boil and simmer for 5 minutes. Process in a blender until smooth. Leave to cool, then refrigerate.

Salt

Babies should not have any added salt until they are one year old, because their kidneys are too immature to cope with it. After a year, try and keep salt to a minimum in their diet. When cooking a family meal you can do this by taking out your child's portion before adding seasoning, if practical. Salt is added to many commercially processed foods such as crisps and other pre-salted snack foods, and stock cubes, so be careful that you aren't giving your child salt unintentionally by including these foods in their diet, and always check the labels of any processed food you buy.

Although some first foods such as baby rice and purées may taste bland to an adult palate, remember that your baby is tasting them for the first time, and their flavour will be very strong compared to the milk they are used to. British adults consume about 9g of salt per day when the recommended maximum is 6g, so getting the whole family to cut down is not a bad idea. It's up to you whether you use salt when cooking recipes from this book. Some of them will definitely need seasoning (unless you are giving them to a child under one, of course), whereas you might find with others that you can get away without any salt at all. It is always better to confine the salt to cooking than adding it later to the plate.

Food Additives

Food additives have been associated with skin complaints, behavioural problems, asthma and many other medical conditions in young children, who are particularly vulnerable to them. Avoiding additives completely is difficult – the only way is to make sure that everything your child eats is fresh and unprocessed. Though having an E number means that an ingredient has passed certain EU safety tests, it doesn't mean that it is any good for us or our children. Colours, preservatives, antioxidants, stabilisers, flavour enhancers, glazing agents and artificial flavourings should all be avoided if possible. Even products that come with reassuring health claims such as 'no artificial colours or preservatives' may well contain artificial flavourings. 'No added sugar' may mean the product contains chemical sweeteners such as saccharin or aspartane, which are banned from foods for children under twelve months and have been linked with serious health problems. When shopping for food, the best strategy is to read the label and go for products that contain a short list of identifiable ingredients. Avoid anything you don't recognise as food – for example, acidity regulator, glucono delta-lactone or maltodextrin. You and your children definitely don't need these in your diet.

Sugar and salt are added to many processed foods unnecessarily so that children (and adults) will find them more palatable. Sugar can be associated with behavioural problems, so if your child is sensitive to it, avoid processed foods. It may be deceptively labelled under many other names such as sucrose, glucose, fructose, glucose syrup and corn syrup. Fructose, the natural sugar present in fruit, is slowly absorbed as energy when eaten in fruit but if it is separated from the fruit fibre and turned into, say, a fruit-flavoured drink, it is absorbed like any refined sugar. Honey and brown sugar have healthier connotations but they too are absorbed in exactly the same way as refined sugar so they do not present an acceptable alternative.

Freezing Children's Foods

Certain foods freeze better than others. Purées, sauces, soups and most meat and fish dishes generally freeze well, although some dishes containing garlic don't. Thawed frozen food should not be refrozen unless it has been thoroughly cooked – for example, if you use frozen uncooked meat to make a shepherd's pie or frozen peas to make a purée. When preparing foods to go in the freezer, cook them thoroughly, cool them down as quickly as possible, then package them for freezing when completely cold. For small babies, freeze purées in sterilised ice-cube trays and, when frozen, knock out the cubes and put them into freezer bags clearly labelled with the contents and the expiry date. Larger containers can be used for older babies and toddlers, but check that they are suitable for the freezer as some containers may shatter below certain temperatures.

When defrosting frozen foods, either thaw them as quickly as possible at room temperature or, better still, defrost overnight in the fridge. Reheat foods thoroughly and serve immediately or cool them down for younger babies. Throw away anything that has not been used within 24 hours.

Freezer Storage Times

Fruit and vegetables: max 6 months
Soups or purées with milk or cream: max 2 months
Fish (either raw or made up into dishes): max 3 months
Meat/poultry (either raw or made up into dishes): max 3 months

Equipment

If you have a well-equipped kitchen then you probably already possess everything you need to prepare food for babies and small children. A good-quality blender is useful for purées and soups, although for younger babies you will need to sieve them afterwards as well. There are some great mini food processors and hand-held blenders on the market now which make light work of small quantities of purées.

Rubber spatulas are very useful for getting to the bottom of the blender and food processor and for scraping out bowls and pans.

Stainless-steel sieves and strainers in various sizes will get rid of unwanted pips, seeds and skin. Good-quality stainless-steel saucepans stay clean and can go in the dishwasher, which helps to sterilise them.

From a safety point of view, ensure that your knives are sharp as, believe it or not, a blunt knife is more dangerous than a sharp one because it is more likely to slip on the chopping board.

A deep-fat fryer is a good investment if you enjoy fried food. Because it is thermostatically controlled and has a lid, it is safer to use than a saucepan. If the pan is not too crowded and the oil is very hot, the food absorbs less fat and is not as calorific as you might imagine.

Soups and Stocks

57 Vegetable Stock

57 Chicken Stock

59 Carrot and Cumin Soup

59 Tomato Soup

61 Minted Pea Soup

61 Chicken and Sweetcorn Soup

63 Chicken, Vegetable and Lentil Broth

63 Melon Soup

63 Iced Strawberry Soup with Fromage Frais

Soup is the ultimate comfort food. It is also one of the easiest ways to get small children to eat fresh vegetables. You can make it thick and satisfying for a wintry supper, light and fresh in spring, or chilled and fruity for an unusual summer pudding. Anything goes. Thick soups are easier and less messy for a small child to eat if you don't want to redecorate the kitchen afterwards. If necessary, take a ladleful of solids out of the cooked soup and purée it separately for your child (a hand-held blender makes this easy to achieve) before blending the rest for adults.

Soups should taste of their ingredients. On the whole they don't require much cooking. Vegetable soups that are to be puréed only need cooking for as long as it takes to soften the vegetables, otherwise they lose their fresh flavour.

A good soup starts with good stock. Do have a go at making your own. It doesn't take nearly as long as you might imagine and it's a great way to use up bones and vegetable trimmings (but not leftover vegetables that have already been cooked and lost their flavour). It's worth making a large batch of stock and freezing it. If you are short of freezer space, boil the stock to reduce it to a concentrate, then freeze in ice-cube trays. Use a few cubes at a time, adding water to make them up to their original volume. If you don't have time to make your own stock, there are alternatives. Supermarkets now sell good, albeit expensive, fresh stocks, and Marigold stock concentrate is a useful substitute.

Vegetable Stock

Suitable for: 4 months +
Makes about 3 litres

5 onions, peeled and roughly chopped
1kg carrots, peeled and roughly chopped
500g leeks, roughly chopped
1 small head of celery, roughly chopped
1 teaspoon black peppercorns
1 teaspoon fennel seeds
2 bay leaves
2 sprigs of thyme
5 cloves of garlic, peeled and roughly chopped

Put all the ingredients into a large pot, cover with plenty of cold water and bring to the boil. Simmer for 40–50 minutes, skimming any scum from the surface if necessary. Strain through a fine sieve. Taste and check the strength; if it is a little weak, reduce it by boiling to concentrate the flavour.

Store in the fridge for 3–4 days or freeze.

Chicken Stock

Suitable for: 6 months +
Makes about 3 litres

1kg chicken bones, chopped
3 medium leeks, roughly chopped
3 medium onions, peeled and roughly chopped
1/2 head of celery, roughly chopped
2 sprigs of thyme
1 bay leaf
1 teaspoon black peppercorns

Wash the chicken bones to remove any blood. Put them into a large pot with the rest of the ingredients and cover with plenty of cold water (about 5 litres). Bring to the boil, skim off any scum that forms on top and simmer very gently for about $1^1/_2$–2 hours. During cooking, you may need to add more water to keep the ingredients covered; skim occasionally if necessary.

Strain the stock through a fine sieve and remove any fat from the surface with a ladle. Or you can chill it and then lift the solidified fat off the top. Taste and check the strength; if it is a little weak, reduce it by boiling to concentrate the flavour.

Store in the fridge for 3–4 days or freeze.

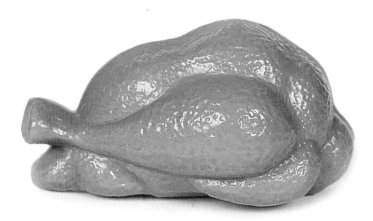

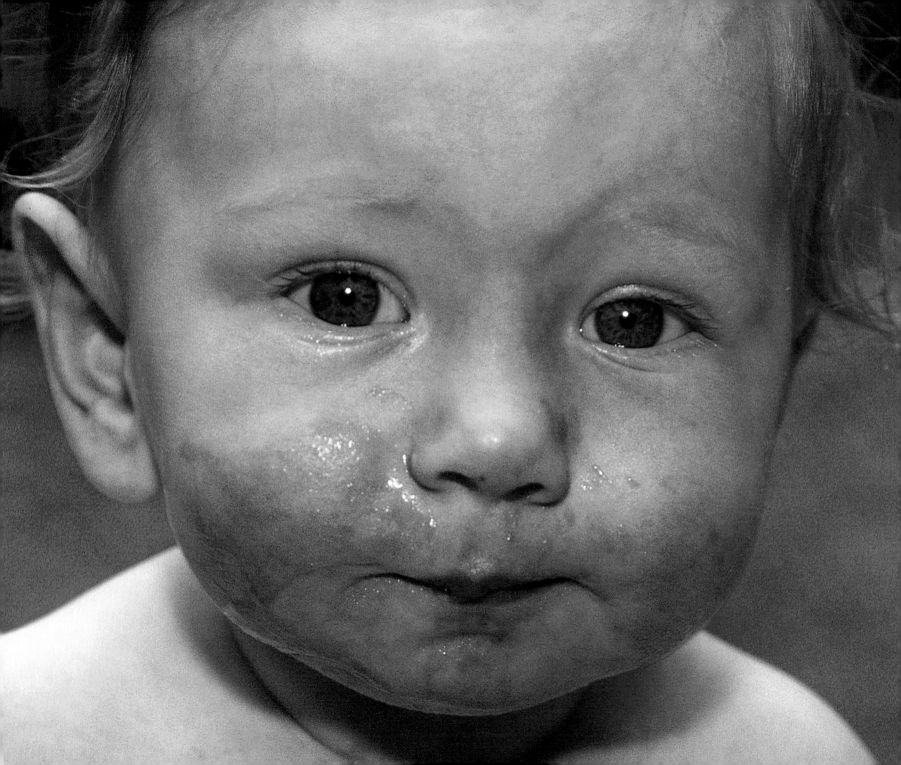

Carrot and Cumin Soup

I love cooking with cumin. In fact it seems to be a standing joke at work that I put it in everything. I find it acts as a seasoning in certain dishes without overspicing them.

Serves 2 adults and 2 small children
Suitable for: 6 months + (omit seasoning for babies)

1 small onion, peeled and roughly chopped
8–10 medium carrots, peeled and roughly chopped
1 teaspoon cumin seeds
Leaves from a few sprigs of thyme
2 tablespoons olive oil
1 litre vegetable stock

Gently cook the onion, carrots, cumin seeds and thyme in the olive oil for about 10 minutes, until the vegetables begin to soften. Add the vegetable stock, bring to the boil and simmer for 30 minutes. Purée in a blender until smooth, then strain through a fine sieve. Season with salt and pepper to taste.

Tomato Soup

Always try to buy overripe tomatoes for soup as they will give it that rich tomato sweetness.

Serves 2 adults and 2 small children
Suitable for: 6 months + (omit seasoning for babies)

1 onion, peeled and roughly chopped
1 carrot, peeled and roughly chopped
1 clove of garlic, peeled and crushed
Leaves from a few sprigs of thyme
2 tablespoons olive oil
1 tablespoon tomato purée
500–600g ripe tomatoes, chopped
1 tablespoon plain flour
1 litre vegetable stock
A handful of basil, finely chopped

Gently cook the onion, carrot, garlic and thyme in the olive oil for about 5 minutes, until they begin to soften. Add the tomato purée, tomatoes and flour, stir well and cook for 2 minutes. Gradually stir in the vegetable stock, then bring to the boil and simmer for 45–50 minutes. Purée in a blender until smooth, then pass through a fine sieve. Stir in the basil and season with salt and pepper to taste.

Minted Pea Soup

I prefer to use frozen peas because they have a consistently sweet flavour and are much more convenient. Quite often, after all the labour of shelling them, fresh peas turn out to be tough and flavourless when they are cooked.

Serves 2 adults and 2 small children
Suitable for: 6 months +
(omit seasoning – and bacon if you're using it – for babies)

2 tablespoons vegetable oil
1 onion, peeled and finely chopped
1 small leek, trimmed and roughly chopped
2 rashers of bacon, chopped (optional)
500g frozen peas
2 sprigs of fresh mint
1 litre vegetable stock

Heat the vegetable oil in a large pan, add the onion, leek and bacon, if using, and cook gently until the vegetables are soft. Add the peas, mint and stock, bring to the boil and simmer for 10 minutes. Purée in a blender and then strain in a fine sieve. Season with salt and pepper to taste.

Chicken and Sweetcorn Soup

Everyone loves sweetcorn. I find frozen or canned is best for purées or soups because of the consistency of flavour. If you reduce the amount of stock and don't purée this soup, it becomes a hearty stew for adults and older children.

Serves 2 adults and 2 small children
Suitable for: 8 months + (omit seasoning for babies)

2 chicken thighs, skinned and boned
1 litre chicken stock
30g unsalted butter
1 onion, peeled and roughly chopped
1 leek, roughly chopped
300g tinned or frozen sweetcorn
2–4 tablespoons double cream (optional)

Put the chicken thighs in a pan with enough of the stock to cover, bring to the boil and simmer for 10 minutes or until cooked through. Remove from the liquid, leave to cool and reserve the stock.

While the chicken is cooking, heat the butter in a pan and gently cook the onion and leek for 2–3 minutes, without colouring, until soft. Add the sweetcorn and the stock (including the stock in which the chicken was cooked), bring to the boil and simmer for 15 minutes. Purée in a blender, then strain through a fine sieve.

Chop the chicken finely – as small as you can for babies – and add to the soup, together with the cream, if using. Season with salt and pepper to taste, reheat and serve.

Chicken, Vegetable and Lentil Broth

A colourful way to get children used to different textures and flavours. Chicken thighs are used as they have a better flavour than breasts and withstand longer cooking. Other vegetables such as potato, celeriac and French beans could be added.

Serves 2 adults and 2 small children
Suitable for: 9 months + (omit seasoning for babies)

80g Puy lentils
2 tablespoons olive oil
2 chicken thighs, skinned, boned and cut into 1cm dice
1 small onion, peeled and finely chopped
2 carrots, peeled and cut into 1cm dice
150g swede, peeled and cut into 1cm dice
1 clove of garlic, peeled and crushed
Leaves from a few sprigs of thyme, finely chopped
500ml chicken stock
A few sprigs of parsley, finely chopped

Cook the lentils in boiling water for 30–40 minutes, until tender. Meanwhile, in a separate pan, heat the olive oil and gently cook the chicken, vegetables, garlic and thyme for a couple of minutes without colouring them. Add the chicken stock, bring to the boil and simmer for 45–50 minutes. Drain the lentils, add them to the soup with the parsley, then simmer for another 10 minutes. Season with salt and pepper to taste.

Melon Soup

Always use the sweetest melons available – Galia, Charentais, cantaloupe etc – add some watermelon for colour, if available.

Suitable for: 5 months +

Simply peel and deseed the melon and purée in a blender until smooth. Chill for 1–2 hours, or put in the freezer if you're in a hurry. Grown-ups can add a little Campari and grenadine to their portion for an extra sensation. Don't get them mixed up though.

Iced Strawberry Soup with Fromage Frais

A simple summer soup that everyone will enjoy. Eat it with a spoon or drink it through a straw. It can also be served as a dessert, but children might enjoy the fact that they are getting their pudding first for a change.

Serves 2 adults and 2 small children
Suitable for: 6 months +

400g ripe strawberries, hulled
Leaves from 1 sprig of mint
About 2 tablespoons caster sugar, depending on the
  sweetness of the strawberries
100g fromage frais

Purée the strawberries in a blender with the mint leaves and sugar until smooth. Transfer to a shallow bowl and place in the freezer for about an hour, until semi-frozen, stirring occasionally. Serve in a soup bowl or cups, topping each portion with a spoonful of the fromage frais.

Vegetables and Salads

71 Cumin-roasted Sweet Vegetables
71 Aubergine Escalopes with Melted Mozzarella
73 Caribbean Vegetable Hot-pot
73 Sweet Potato Rösti
75 Proper Mashed Potato
75 Colcannon
77 Chips
77 Parmesan and Rosemary Baked
    Potato Wedges
79 Buttery Sugarsnaps with Smoky Bacon
79 Cumin-spiced Lentils with Coriander
81 Home-made Baked Beans
81 Gratin of Broccoli with Mascarpone
    and Parmesan
83 Little Gems with Thousand Island Dressing
83 Couscous and Herb Salad
85 Greek Salad
85 Crushed Potato Mayonnaise
87 Vegetable Purées
87 Roast Pumpkin and Ginger Purée
89 Pea Purée
89 Celeriac and Apple Mash
91 Bashed Neeps
91 Tim's Carrot Purée with Basil

Very few children can make a convincing rejection of all vegetables nowadays. There is an astonishing range to choose from, and some of the relatively new arrivals in the shops, such as butternut squash, sweet potatoes and tiny cherry tomatoes, seem designed expressly to appeal to a naturally sweet-toothed small child. Today's kids are lucky that they can take all this variety for granted. When I was a child, new potatoes were something that came out of cans but now at least eight varieties of waxy potatoes, with well-brought-up names like Charlotte, are the norm in any supermarket. Mangetout, and recently the even racier sugarsnap, have supplanted those grey hailstone peas that used to accompany every school meal. Previously exotic items such as avocado, okra and yams are commonplace. Courgettes, *the* luxury item not very long ago, now come in a bewildering range of colours and shapes, and people can't make up their minds whether they're called courgette or zucchini.

If your children aren't keen on boiled or steamed vegetables it's time to rethink your cooking method. Roasting is usually a good choice. It brings out the natural sweetness of vegetables and results in a crisp outside and a tender, meltingly soft interior – use the recipe for Cumin-roasted Vegetables on page 71 as a blueprint. Frying provides an appealing crispness too, and recipes such as Sweet Potato Rösti on page 73 don't use a lot of oil. Vegetable purées and mashes make perfect comfort food and can be enriched with cheese or enlivened with gentle spices such as ginger. A good way of getting children to eat lettuce is by serving it with Thousand Island Dressing (see page 83), which many find irresistible – try using it as a dip for raw vegetables as well.

All children have different tastes, of course, so be prepared for disasters as well as triumphs. Try the recipes in this chapter and don't give up if they reject them at first – just experiment with other ingredients. Sweet Potato Rösti, for example, are just as tasty made with a non-sweet, plain old spud, and cauliflower can be substituted for broccoli in the Broccoli and Mascarpone Gratin on page 81.

Cumin-roasted Sweet Vegetables

Roasting vegetables gives an extra dimension to the sometimes bland flavours that boiling and steaming can produce. The vegetables suggested below can be replaced by your own favourites if you prefer.

Serves 2 adults and 2 small children
Suitable for: 9 months + (omit seasoning for babies)

3 tablespoons olive oil
1 small butternut squash, peeled, deseeded and cut into small, rough shapes
1 small sweet potato, peeled and cut into small, rough shapes
2 parsnips, peeled and cut into small, rough shapes
$1/2$ teaspoon ground cumin
$1/2$ teaspoon cumin seeds
Leaves from a few sprigs of thyme, chopped

Heat the olive oil in a large heavy frying pan, then add the vegetables and cook them over a high heat for a few minutes until lightly browned, turning them with a spoon. Stir in the cumin and thyme, then transfer to a roasting tray or, if the pan has a metal handle, put it straight into the oven. Cook for 20–25 minutes in an oven preheated to 200°C/Gas Mark 6, turning occasionally, until tender, then season with salt and pepper to taste.

Aubergine Escalopes with Melted Mozzarella

This makes an interesting vegetarian main course or starter, or serve it as an antipasto or as part of a buffet. Try to buy buffalo mozzarella as there is no comparison between that and the plastic substitutes.

Serves 2 adults and 2 small children
Suitable for: 18 months +

Flour seasoned with salt and pepper, for dusting
2 small free-range eggs, beaten
60g fresh white breadcrumbs, mixed with 60g freshly grated Parmesan cheese
2 large or 3 small aubergines, cut into slices 1–1.5cm thick
4 tablespoons vegetable oil
Pomodoro sauce (see page 101)
150–200g good-quality mozzarella, cut into slices 5mm thick

Have ready 4 dishes. Put the flour in the first, the beaten eggs in the second and the breadcrumbs and Parmesan in the third. The fourth is for the prepared aubergine. Coat the aubergine pieces with the flour, then the egg and lastly the breadcrumb mixture. Make sure you shake off any excess flour before dipping the aubergine in the egg, or the breadcrumbs will not stick.

Heat the vegetable oil in a frying pan and cook the aubergine slices for a couple of minutes on each side, until golden and tender. You will probably need to do them in batches. Lay them on a grill tray and place a couple of teaspoons of pomodoro sauce on top of each one, followed by a slice of mozzarella. Grill the aubergines until the mozzarella just melts.

Caribbean Vegetable Hot-pot

The sweet flavours of plantain, yam and sweet potato make this an easy way to introduce children to the concept of stew. It makes a great vegetarian main course or can be served as an accompaniment to grilled or roast meat.

Serves 2 adults and 2 small children
Suitable for: 9 months + (omit seasoning and chilli for babies)

1 onion, peeled and chopped
30g root ginger, scraped and finely chopped
1 clove of garlic, peeled and crushed
$^1/_2$ teaspoon cumin seeds
1 mild chilli, seeded and finely chopped (optional)
2 tablespoons vegetable oil
200g sweet potato, peeled and diced
200g yam, peeled and diced
1 litre vegetable stock
1 small plantain, peeled, cut in half lengthways and sliced
100g okra, thinly sliced
1 tablespoon finely chopped fresh coriander

Gently cook the onion, ginger, garlic, cumin seeds and chilli, if using, in the vegetable oil until soft. Add the sweet potato, yam and vegetable stock and simmer for 20 minutes. Add the plantain and okra and simmer for another 10 minutes or until the vegetables are tender. The liquid should have thickened and reduced by now; if it has reduced too much, add a little more stock. Stir in the coriander and simmer for 5 minutes, then season with salt and pepper to taste.

Sweet Potato Rösti

These little potato pancakes are good served with apple sauce and soured cream, or even with tomato ketchup. For adults and older children, they go very well with Continental-style sausages and fried eggs.

Serves 2 adults and 2 small children
Suitable for: 9 months + (omit seasoning for babies)

3–4 sweet potatoes, weighing about 250–300g each
1 onion, peeled and thinly sliced
Vegetable oil for frying

Put the sweet potatoes in a saucepan, cover with water and bring to the boil, then simmer for 15 minutes, so they are partly cooked. Drain and leave to cool – under the cold tap is quickest. Peel the potatoes by scraping off the skin with a knife, then grate or shred them with a mandolin, a grater or the grating attachment of a food processor. Put into a bowl and mix with the sliced onion and some salt and pepper.

Heat a little vegetable oil in a large frying pan. Dollop in spoonfuls of the sweet potato mixture, flattening them with the back of a spoon. Cook for 2–3 minutes on each side, until crisp.

Proper Mashed Potato

Although a simple dish, mashed potato can go horribly wrong. First, it's important to buy the correct potatoes. Waxy ones are no good at all; you will end up with a pan full of glue. Try to buy floury, well-flavoured potatoes such as King Edward or Maris Piper.

I often used to wonder why the restaurant's mash sometimes lacked flavour, despite being made with good potatoes. So I developed a method where we slowly bake the potatoes in their skins at about 170°C/Gas Mark 3, then scoop out the flesh and mash it as normal, which gives a consistently earthy mash. This method does take longer – 1–2 hours if using a conventional oven – but you could use a microwave, which will take 10–15 minutes. I have given the standard boiling method below but, should you use the baking method, just get the potatoes on well in advance.

Serves 2 adults and 2 small children
Suitable for: 9 months + (omit seasoning for babies)

500–600g potatoes, peeled and cut into even-sized pieces
3 tablespoons full-cream milk
3 tablespoons cream
A knob of butter

Put the potatoes in a saucepan, cover with water and bring to the boil, then simmer until tender; test with a knife. Drain the potatoes through a colander, then return to the pan and place on a low heat for a minute to evaporate any excess water.

Mash the potatoes – you can use either a potato masher or the grater attachment of a food processor – then push them through a sieve. Alternatively a potato ricer, which looks like a giant garlic press, is the perfect gadget. Bring the milk, cream and butter to the boil in a small pan, then beat into the potato and season to taste.

Colcannon

A simple Irish country dish that's perfect for young children and can be enjoyed on its own or as an accompaniment to most meat dishes. You could also serve it topped with a poached egg or add some chopped ham to make it more substantial.

Serves 2 adults and 2 small children
Suitable for: 9 months +
 (omit seasoning – and butter if you like – for babies)

150–180g green cabbage, finely chopped
4 spring onions, finely chopped
1 quantity of Proper Mashed Potato (see left)
A large knob of butter, melted

Cook the cabbage in boiling salted water until tender, adding the spring onions about a minute before the cabbage is cooked. Drain well and mix with the mashed potato. Season to taste, then transfer to 4 individual dishes, make a little hollow in the centre of each portion and fill with melted butter. The idea is to take a forkful of the potato mixture and dip it in the butter.

Chips

Suitable for: 1 year +

There are all sorts of different chip cutters these days, so if you want *pommes allumettes* (fine cut) or chips (thick cut), use the appropriate attachment or gadget. Alternatively you can, of course, simply use a good sharp knife.

Allow 200–250g of potatoes per person. Peel them, square the ends off and then, for thick-cut chips, cut each potato into 1cm slices, then cut the slices into chips 1cm thick. Prepare thinly cut chips in the same way but cut to 5mm. Wash the chips well to remove the starch, then dry on kitchen paper.

The secret of good chips is to fry them twice – once at a low temperature to soften them, then briefly at a higher temperature until crisp and golden. Heat some oil to 130°C in a deep-fat fryer and fry the chips two or three handfuls at a time until they are soft but not coloured. Remove from the oil and drain on kitchen paper. You can store the chips in this state in the fridge for up to a couple of days.

To serve the chips, re-fry them at 180°C until crisp, drain on kitchen paper and season lightly with salt.

Parmesan and Rosemary Baked Potato Wedges

Suitable for: 1 year +

A good alternative to chips. Simply cut some large potatoes into wedges with the skin on. Pour a thin layer of olive oil into a roasting tin and put in an oven preheated to 220°C/Gas Mark 7 for a few minutes. Add the potatoes, then place in the oven and cook, turning every so often, for about 40 minutes. Scatter some freshly grated Parmesan and some rosemary leaves over the potatoes and return to the oven for another 10 minutes.

Buttery Sugarsnaps with Smoky Bacon

Sugarsnaps appeal to me more than mangetout. They are a bit more substantial and are full of tiny peas, which kids love.

Serves 2 adults and 2 small children
Suitable for: 1 year +

90g rindless smoked streaky bacon, finely diced
A little vegetable oil
200g sugarsnaps
A pinch of sugar
30g butter

Gently fry the bacon in a little vegetable oil for a few minutes without letting it colour too much. Meanwhile, in a separate pan, just cover the sugarsnaps with boiling water, add the sugar, butter, and some salt and pepper if you want, and bring back to the boil. Cook on a high heat for 2–3 minutes, until the sugarsnaps are just tender and the liquid has almost evaporated. Add the bacon, stir well and serve immediately.

Cumin-spiced Lentils with Coriander

I think it's important to introduce young children to spices as early as possible. Spice does not have to mean heat. Cumin, my favourite spice, has a rather addictive flavour and can be used in all sorts of dishes without being hot.

Serve these spiced lentils with basmati rice, with poppadums or naan bread, or with grilled meats. A spoonful of yoghurt can be stirred in at the end to give a creamier finish.

Serves 2 adults and 2 small children
Suitable for: 9 months + (omit seasoning for babies)

1 onion, peeled and finely chopped
2 cloves of garlic, peeled and crushed
2 teaspoons finely grated root ginger
2 teaspoons ground cumin
$^1/_2$ teaspoon cumin seeds
1 teaspoon ground turmeric
1 tablespoon vegetable oil
2 teaspoons tomato purée
200g yellow or red lentils.
  Soaking them in cold water for 1 hour, then draining,
  shortens the cooking time
400–450ml vegetable stock
1 tablespoon chopped fresh coriander

Gently cook the onion, garlic, ginger and spices in the vegetable oil until soft. Add the tomato purée, lentils and vegetable stock, bring to the boil and simmer for 35–40 minutes, until the lentils are almost falling apart and the liquid has evaporated. If it evaporates before the lentils are cooked, add more stock or water.

Stir in the coriander and simmer for 5 minutes, then add salt and pepper to taste.

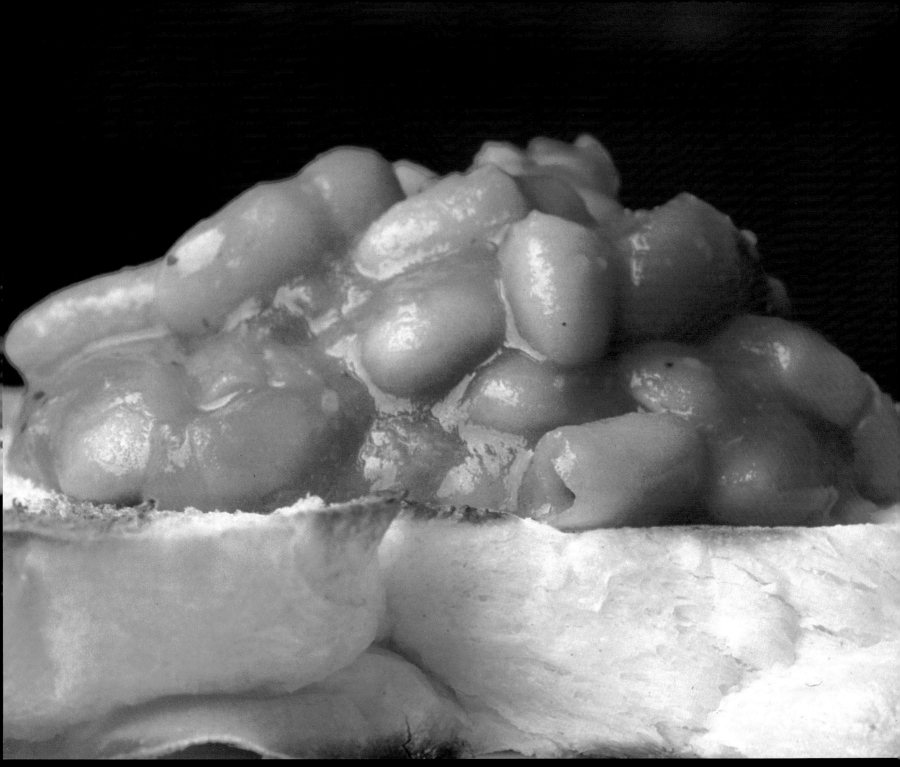

Home-made Baked Beans

For all the obvious reasons, making your own baked beans is better than buying them. Home-made ones are completely natural and the flavour is true to the ingredients, unlike the commercial equivalent. You can also experiment with the type of beans you use – try chickpeas, blackeye beans or flageolets.

Serves 2 adults and 2 small children
Suitable for: 9 months + (omit seasoning for babies)

1 onion, peeled and finely chopped
1 clove of garlic, peeled and crushed
Leaves from a few sprigs of thyme, chopped
2 tablespoons vegetable oil
2 tablespoons tomato purée
6 large, firm tomatoes, skinned and chopped, or about 200g
    tinned chopped tomatoes
2 teaspoons caster sugar
400g tin of haricot beans or similar, drained and rinsed
200ml vegetable stock

Gently cook the onion, garlic and thyme in the vegetable oil until soft. Add the tomato purée, tomatoes, sugar, haricot beans and stock. Bring to the boil and simmer for 30–35 minutes, stirring occasionally. Add a little water if the liquid evaporates too soon. Season with salt and pepper to taste.

Gratin of Broccoli with Mascarpone and Parmesan

Mascarpone is a type of rich cream cheese. It is very versatile and can be used where you would normally use cream or crème fraîche.

This simple sauce can be served with other vegetables such as leeks, cauliflower or broad beans, or serve it with pasta or gnocchi (see page 107) for a quick last-minute meal, assuming you have mascarpone in your fridge.

Serves 2 adults and 2 small children
Suitable for: 6 months + (purée the mixture for babies)

250g broccoli, cut into florets
150g mascarpone cheese
120g Parmesan cheese, freshly grated
30g fresh white breadcrumbs

Cook the broccoli in lightly salted boiling water until tender, then drain well. Meanwhile, bring the mascarpone to the boil, add 90g of the Parmesan and stir until dissolved.

For young babies, mix the broccoli and sauce together and purée in a food processor. For older children and adults, mix the sauce and broccoli together, season lightly with salt and pepper and put into an ovenproof dish. Sprinkle with the remaining Parmesan and the breadcrumbs and grill until golden.

Little Gems with Thousand Island Dressing

When I first arrived in London I frequently visited American and Tex Mex restaurants. I discovered Thousand Island dressing and have been hooked on it ever since. It perks up crisp but bland lettuces and, best of all, it tastes as if you are eating a prawn cocktail without the prawns.

Serves 2 adults and 2 small children
Suitable for: 18 months +

100ml good-quality mayonnaise
1 tablespoon tomato ketchup
1 gherkin, finely chopped
1 chilli, seeded and finely chopped (optional)
1 teaspoon chilli sauce (optional)
1 spring onion, finely chopped
3 Little Gem lettuces, shredded

Put all the ingredients except the lettuce in a bowl and whisk together to make the dressing. If it is too thick, dilute with a little water. Put the lettuce into a serving bowl and pour over the dressing.

Couscous and Herb Salad

A simple salad to make and a good opportunity to introduce young tastebuds to herbs. A traditional Arabic tabbouleh is composed of roughly chopped herbs and very little grain, but I've toned down the herbs and chopped them finely so they are less pungent and more digestible. Serve this as an accompaniment to Koftas (see page 175) or as a light snack. Finely diced cucumber could also be added.

Serves 2 adults and 2 small children
Suitable for: 9 months + (omit seasoning for babies)

60g couscous
Juice of 1 lemon
1/2 bunch of spring onions, finely chopped
4 ripe tomatoes, skinned, deseeded and finely chopped
4 tablespoons finely chopped parsley
4 tablespoons finely chopped mint,
2 tablespoons hot water
4 tablespoons extra virgin olive oil

Mix all the ingredients together, season with salt and pepper, then put into a covered bowl and leave to stand for 1 hour; the couscous will soften and plump up. Stir well, then serve.

Greek Salad

A good Greek salad is as colourful and healthy as you can get. I used to hate the idea of it, probably because I had never had an authentic one. I also hated olives and couldn't bear the thought of olive oil. Now I use it by the gallon.

Chop the vegetables as finely as you wish, depending on the size of the mouths you are feeding. Greek feta can sometimes be a bit salty, so you may want to leave it out or replace it with a milder crumbly cheese such as Lancashire.

Serves 2 adults and 2 small children
Suitable for: 18 months +

¹/₂ cucumber, halved lengthways,
  deseeded and cut into 1cm cubes
4 ripe beef tomatoes, skinned and cut into 1cm cubes
15–20 black olives, stoned and quartered
160–200g good-quality feta cheese, cut into 1cm cubes
A few sprigs of mint, finely chopped
A few sprigs of parsley, finely chopped
4 tablespoons extra virgin olive oil
Juice of 1 lemon

Mix all the ingredients together. Leave to stand at room temperature for an hour or so, then serve with pitta or flat bread.

Crushed Potato Mayonnaise

A simple way of making an easily digestible potato salad. Potato salad is often made with chilled old potatoes and has no flavour. Using freshly cooked, slightly warm waxy potatoes gives it a new lease of life.

Serves 2 adults and 2 small children
Suitable for: 9 months + (omit seasoning for babies)

400–500g small waxy potatoes
4 tablespoons good-quality mayonnaise
1 tablespoon finely chopped chives
1 tablespoon finely chopped parsley

Cook the potatoes in their skins in lightly salted boiling water for 20–25 minutes or until tender. Drain, then cool slightly in some cold water and remove the skins with a small knife.

Mash the potatoes coarsely with a fork or potato masher. Fold in the mayonnaise and herbs, then season to taste with salt and pepper.

Vegetable Purées

Just because vegetables are puréed or mashed it doesn't mean they are only suitable for babies. Purées are nursery food in its most basic form but they also make great accompaniments to main dishes such as braised meat or fish.

I won't give a long list of purée recipes because the method is pretty much the same whatever you are making; use Celeriac and Apple Mash (page 89), as a guideline. You could steam the vegetables instead of boiling them, however, or even roast them for a new flavour. Other good flavour combinations are: carrot and orange; swede and parsnip; broccoli and Parmesan; roasted cauliflower; or fruit purées such as apple and blackberry, banana and pear, etc.

Roast Pumpkin and Ginger Purée

I don't remember squash and pumpkin being used in cooking when I was younger, but once I discovered them I became addicted to their flavour and versatility.

Serves 2 adults and 2 small children
Suitable for: 8 months + (omit seasoning for babies)

Olive oil
500g yellow-fleshed pumpkin or butternut squash, peeled, deseeded and roughly chopped
40g fresh root ginger, peeled and finely grated
A knob of butter

Pour a thin layer of olive oil into a roasting tin and put in an oven preheated to 190°C/Gas Mark 5 for a few minutes. Season the pumpkin pieces, add to the roasting tin and return to the oven for 20–30 minutes or until soft. Meanwhile, simmer the ginger in a small pan of water for 5 minutes, then drain.

Purée the pumpkin in a food processor or blender with the ginger. Finish with the butter and then adjust the seasoning if necessary.

Pea Purée

This is something I developed about nine years ago to go with fish and chips. A lot of our customers enjoy it as a side order and it has become a mainstay in all three restaurants. It also naturally makes ideal nursery food. The colour and wonderfully fresh flavour are very appealing and most people have a bag of peas to hand in their freezer. Don't try and improve on it by using fresh peas; the end result may be disappointing, since the skins of fresh peas can sometimes be tough and they are often less sweet.

Serves 2 adults and 2 small children
Suitable for: 6 months + (omit seasoning for babies)

20g butter, plus a knob of butter to finish
$1/2$ small onion, peeled and finely chopped
500g frozen peas
100ml vegetable stock
A large sprig of mint

Heat the butter in a pan and cook the onion gently until soft. Add the peas, vegetable stock and mint leaves and simmer for 10–12 minutes. Purée in a food processor or blender; if the peas do not purée properly, stop the machine, add a little water and re-blend. Season to taste and finish with the knob of butter.

Celeriac and Apple Mash

Celeriac is very versatile but, unfortunately, not used a lot in the home. It is simple to cook, purées very well and makes a perfect first solids option or accompaniment to main meals.

Serves 2 adults and 2 small children
Suitable for: 4 months +

1 head of celeriac, peeled and cut into chunks
2 eating apples, peeled, cored and cut into chunks

Cover the celeriac and apple with cold water, bring to the boil and simmer for 10–15 minutes, until tender. Purée in a blender, then strain through a sieve for very young babies.

Bashed Neeps

Ideal nursery food, not only for toddlers but also for grown-ups. Serve with Shepherd's Pie (see page 121) or any hearty winter dish.

Serves 2 adults and 2 small children
Suitable for: 6 months + (omit seasoning for babies)

300g swede, peeled and roughly chopped
300g parsnips, peeled and roughly chopped
A knob of butter (optional)

Put the swede and parsnips into a pan, cover with cold water and bring to the boil, then simmer for 15–20 minutes, until soft. Process in a blender or food processor until smooth. Stir in the butter if you're using it, and season with salt and pepper to taste.

Tim's Carrot Purée with Basil

Tim Hughes is my head chef at J. Sheekey. He has twins, too, Rebecca and Jamie – there must be something in the water. This is a simple and quick purée, with the basil and Parmesan adding a Mediterranean twist.

Serves 2 adults and 2 small children
Suitable for: 6 months + (omit seasoning for babies)

500g medium carrots, peeled and roughly chopped
1 tablespoon chopped basil
60g Parmesan cheese, freshly grated
A knob of butter (optional)

Steam or boil the carrots until very tender, then drain. Add the basil, Parmesan and some seasoning and purée in a blender or food processor until smooth. Finish with the butter, if you like.

Eggs, Pasta and Rice

99 Spanish Tortilla
99 Coddled Eggs
101 Scrambled Eggs with Chicken Livers
101 Pasta Pomodoro
103 Pasta e Fagioli
103 Penne with Tuna, Tomato and Olive Oil
105 Farfalle with Pesto
105 Giant Pasta Shells with Chicken and Herbs
107 Butternut Squash Risotto
107 Potato Gnocchi
109 Spinach, Leek and Parmesan Risotto
109 Spring Herb Risotto with Courgettes

The classic infant supper of boiled egg and soldiers has the combined attractions of shell smashing, runny yellow messy stuff, tasty buttered toast and a great name. All children love toast and dipping things, so this is a great opportunity to make a nutritious snack in minutes. Freshness and quality are vital with eggs. Try to buy date-stamped organic or free-range ones. If they aren't dated, write the date on each egg with a felt tip pen (or on the box) and throw them away if you don't use them within two weeks.

Starchy foods like pasta and rice are also perfect for young palates and are infinitely versatile. From cream to tomato sauces, rich ragù to fresh herbs, or just plain olive oil or butter, pasta complements an infinite number of ingredients to make a quick and easy meal. Let your children choose the pasta shape, even the colour, and grate cheese over their own plateful. Pastas that are easy for small children to handle include penne, farfalle and rigatoni; spaghetti is messy but fun. I haven't included any filled pasta recipes in this book but if you have a good Italian deli nearby that makes fresh pasta, it should be a reliable source of tortelloni and ravioli. These make good finger food for babies and toddlers and are usually popular with older children too. Rice is underused compared to pasta but shares its appealingly soft but chewy texture and its ability to take on any flavour. Try making stir-fries, pilafs, biryani or, my favourite, gooey risotto.

All these foods are an ideal way of encouraging children to explore different flavours, since their familiarity will reassure even the most conservative child. Here is a case in point. Recently I showed Ellie and Lydia a piece of fresh tuna, which they hated on sight. But when I made it into a simple pasta sauce with chilli and olive oil, they gobbled it up. Now they demand fresh tuna pasta for dinner all the time.

If you cook too much pasta, don't fret. My friend Pat gave me a brilliant tip from an Italian restaurateur: just mix the leftover pasta and sauce with some beaten eggs to make a chunky frittata (flat omelette). Delicious.

Spanish Tortilla

I'm amazed that most people's perception of a Spanish omelette is lots of chopped-up ingredients mixed with beaten egg. I'm not sure where this idea came from but it's far from the simple dish found in Spain. Potatoes, onion and sometimes a herb are all it contains and all it should.

Serves 2 adults and 2 small children
Suitable for: 9 months + (omit seasoning for babies)

2 medium waxy potatoes, peeled and cut into rough 1cm cubes
50g unsalted butter
1 onion, peeled and finely chopped
2 teaspoons finely chopped chives
6 free-range eggs, beaten

Boil the potatoes for about 5 or 6 minutes, until just tender, then drain and set aside. Melt half the butter in a pan and slowly cook the onion until soft and translucent. Melt the remaining butter in a heavy-based 20cm non-stick frying pan. Mix the onion with the potatoes, chives, eggs and some seasoning and pour into the pan. Stir a couple of times, then leave on a low heat for a minute or so, until set. Turn the tortilla with a fish slice, cook for a minute or two longer until set underneath, then slide on to a plate. If you don't want to turn the tortilla, you could just put it briefly under a hot grill to set the top. Serve warm rather than hot.

Coddled Eggs

A fun way to serve eggs cooked in their own little pots. Ellie and Lydia love helping to make their 'special eggs'. They put some chopped ham, cooked bacon, poached fish or creamed mushrooms or spinach in little ramekins before cracking the eggs into them, then once they are cooked they eat them out of the pots.

Suitable for: 1 year +

Grease some ramekins or similar pots with a little unsalted butter. Put a couple of teaspoons of your chosen filling in them, then carefully crack an egg into each dish. Place them in a roasting tin containing about 3cm of boiling water and bake in an oven preheated to 170°C/Gas Mark 3 for 8–10 minutes, until just set. Serve immediately.

Scrambled Eggs with Chicken Livers

Scrambled eggs are a great way of introducing new flavours to your child's diet. One of my favourite ways of serving them to my kids is with breakfast ingredients such as bacon and sausages chopped up and stirred in.

Always remember not to stir scrambled eggs with a metal spoon or they will be grey and metallic-tasting. Use a wooden spoon instead.

Serves 2
Suitable for: 1 year +

1 tablespoon olive oil
60g chicken livers, de-veined, cleaned and finely chopped
2–3 spring onions, finely chopped
A knob of butter
4 free-range eggs, beaten
2 tablespoons double cream or milk

Heat the olive oil in a frying pan and quickly fry the chicken livers and spring onions for a minute or two, stirring occasionally. Drain on kitchen paper. Melt the butter in a small, heavy-based pan. Mix the eggs and cream or milk together, add to the pan and cook on a low heat for 4–5 minutes, stirring constantly with a wooden spoon. When the eggs have thickened and cooked through, stir in the chicken livers and spring onions and reheat for a minute or so. Serve with toast.

Pasta Pomodoro

This fresh tomato sauce is really simple and quick to produce. If you serve it with spaghetti, chop it up into little pieces for a small child as it can be difficult to swallow.

Pomodoro sauce has lots of other uses in the kitchen. It can be served cold as a dip or used as a base for other sauces – added to minced meat to make a quick bolognese, for example. So if you have time, make up a large batch and freeze it in small amounts.

Serves 2 adults and 2 small children
Suitable for: 9 months + (omit seasoning for babies)

200–250g pasta (rigatoni, linguine, spaghetti etc)
A few sprigs of basil, roughly chopped
Freshly grated Parmesan cheese, to serve

For the sauce:
2 tablespoons extra virgin olive oil
1 small onion, peeled and finely chopped
1 clove of garlic, peeled and crushed
Leaves from a few sprigs of thyme, finely chopped
2 teaspoons tomato purée
10 large, firm tomatoes, skinned, deseeded and roughly chopped, or 400g tin of chopped tomatoes

To make the sauce, heat the olive oil in a pan and gently cook the onion, garlic and thyme until softened but not coloured. Add the tomato purée, chopped tomatoes and half a cup of water and simmer gently for 25–30 minutes, until reduced and thickened. Season with salt and pepper to taste.

Meanwhile, cook the pasta in boiling salted water until tender. Drain the pasta and toss with the sauce and fresh basil. Serve with Parmesan cheese.

Pasta e Fagioli

A cross between a stew and a soup, this classic peasant dish of pasta and beans can be enjoyed by all the family because the ingredients are very finely chopped. Like most stews and soups, it benefits from being reheated the following day.

Serves 2 adults and 2 small children
Suitable for: 9 months + (omit seasoning for babies)

1 onion, peeled and finely chopped
2 sticks of celery, peeled and cut into 1cm dice
2 cloves of garlic, peeled and crushed
A few sprigs of rosemary, leaves removed and finely chopped
4 rashers of unsmoked streaky bacon or slices of ham, finely chopped
2 tablespoons olive oil
400g tin of haricot beans, drained
300g tomatoes, skinned, deseeded and chopped, or a 200g tin of chopped tomatoes
600ml vegetable stock
80g small pasta shapes, such as macaroni
A few sprigs of flat-leaf parsley, finely chopped
Freshly grated Parmesan, to serve

Gently cook the onion, celery, garlic, rosemary and bacon or ham in the olive oil for a few minutes until the vegetables are soft. Purée half the beans in a food processor or blender, then add to the pan with the tomatoes and vegetable stock. Bring to the boil and simmer for 40 minutes. Meanwhile, cook the pasta in boiling water until *al dente*, then drain.

Add the cooked pasta, the whole beans and the parsley to the stew and simmer for a further 10–15 minutes. The mixture should have a thick, soup-like consistency; add a little more water or stock if necessary. Season with salt and freshly ground black pepper. It is nice with freshly grated Parmesan and a drizzle of olive oil.

Penne with Tuna, Tomato and Olive Oil

A quick, clean-tasting pasta dish. I sometimes use fresh tuna but it's not really essential. Just buy good-quality tinned tuna in olive oil and use the oil from the tin for the sauce.

Serves 2 adults and 2 small children
Suitable for: 1 year +

200–250g penne
1/2 onion, peeled and finely chopped
1 clove of garlic, peeled and crushed
2 tablespoons olive oil
1 teaspoon tomato purée
2 ripe tomatoes, skinned, deseeded and chopped
200g tin of tuna in olive oil, drained (reserve the oil)

Cook the penne in lightly salted boiling water until just tender. Meanwhile, gently cook the onion and garlic in the olive oil until soft. Add the tomato purée, tomatoes and the oil from the tuna and simmer for 2–3 minutes. Add the tuna to the sauce with 2 tablespoons of water and heat through for 2–3 minutes. If it seems dry, add a little more oil or water. Season with salt and pepper to taste.

Drain the pasta and mix with the sauce, then serve.

Farfalle with Pesto

All sorts of pasta are filling the supermarket shelves these days, which is great for children because you can choose the size and shape to suit their age. And when they get bored with it, just try a different type. Farfalle are bow-tie shapes, which most children seem to find fun, but you could choose whatever you wanted.

Pesto is a good, quick emergency sauce which many children like. You can leave out the nuts if they are an issue. It keeps in the fridge for a month or so, as long as you cover the surface with a thin layer of oil. Besides serving it with pasta, try tossing it with boiled new potatoes, stirring it into cooked rice or adding it to scrambled eggs, omelettes and sandwiches.

Serves 2 adults and 2 small children
Suitable for: 9 months + (omit seasoning for babies)

200–250g farfalle

For the pesto:
100g basil
1 clove of garlic, peeled and crushed
20g pine nuts, lightly toasted (optional)
100ml olive oil
30g Parmesan cheese, freshly grated

To make the pesto, process all the ingredients in a blender to a coarse paste. Season with salt and pepper according to taste.

Cook the pasta in boiling salted water until tender, then drain and mix with enough pesto to bind.

Giant Pasta Shells with Chicken and Herbs

Giant pasta shells are a novelty and most kids will be intrigued when presented with this dish. They are not available in all supermarkets but most Italian delis stock them. Try them with other fillings, such as Tuna Bolognese (see page 141) or simply Pomodoro Sauce (see page 101) and grated cheese.

Serves 2 adults and 2 small children
Suitable for: 1 year +

1 onion, peeled and finely chopped
400g chicken, very finely chopped
1/2 teaspoon finely chopped thyme
1 clove of garlic, peeled and crushed
2 tablespoons vegetable oil
1 tablespoon plain flour
1 tablespoon tomato purée
700ml chicken stock
1 tablespoon finely chopped parsley
150g giant pasta shells
A little freshly grated Parmesan cheese

Fry the onion, chicken, thyme and garlic in the vegetable oil until lightly coloured. Add the flour and tomato purée and stir well. Gradually stir in the chicken stock, bring to the boil and simmer gently for 45 minutes, then stir in the parsley. Meanwhile, cook the pasta shells in lightly salted boiling water until *al dente*, then drain and refresh in cold water.

Put the pasta shells into an ovenproof dish and put a couple of spoonfuls of the filling into each one. Sprinkle a little cheese on top, then bake in an oven preheated to 220°C/Gas Mark 7 for 10–15 minutes, until golden.

Butternut Squash Risotto

The naturally sweet taste and vibrant orange colour of butternut squash make it perfect for a colourful risotto that children instantly take a liking to.

Serves 2 adults and 2 small children
Suitable for: 9 months + (omit seasoning for babies)

800ml vegetable stock
2 teaspoons tomato purée
1 small butternut squash (about 450–500g), peeled, deseeded
  and cut into 1cm dice
1 tablespoon olive oil
200g carnaroli or arborio rice
3 tablespoons finely chopped parsley
4 tablespoons double cream
50g Parmesan cheese, freshly grated

Bring the vegetable stock to the boil with the tomato purée, add the butternut squash and simmer for 3–4 minutes, until tender. Remove the squash with a slotted spoon and set aside. Keep the stock hot.

To make the risotto, heat the olive oil in a heavy-based pan, add the rice and stir over a low heat for a minute or so until it turns translucent. Gradually add the hot stock, a ladleful at a time, stirring constantly and ensuring that it has been fully absorbed by the rice before adding the next batch. After about 20–25 minutes, when the rice is almost cooked (there may be some stock left), add the butternut squash, parsley and cream. Cook for a further 5 minutes, then stir in the Parmesan, season to taste and serve.

Potato Gnocchi

A good alternative to pasta, these little potato dumplings can be served with any pasta sauce. They take a bit of time to make but children usually enjoy helping to shape them. Instead of tossing the cooked gnocchi in butter you could fry them, which makes them nice and crisp, and serve them with a stew or on their own.

Serves 2 adults and 2 small children
Suitable for: 1 year +

500g large floury potatoes
30g plain flour
50g potato flour
1 tablespoon olive oil
2 eggs
1 egg yolk
Freshly grated nutmeg
90g butter
Freshly grated Parmesan cheese, to serve

Bake the potatoes in an oven preheated to 170°C/Gas Mark 3 until tender. Cut them in half, scoop out the flesh and push through a sieve, or use a potato ricer or mouli-légumes. Leave to cool, then mix in all the remaining ingredients except the butter and Parmesan and season to taste. Test the mixture by dropping a couple of teaspoonfuls into a pan of boiling salted water and simmering until they rise to the top. Taste and adjust the seasoning if necessary, or add a little more plain flour if the mixture is too wet.

Mould the mixture into small balls about the size of a hazelnut, then hold a fork, outer curve downwards, on a floured surface and roll each gnocchi over the tines of the fork to shape them and give a slightly corrugated effect. Rest the gnocchi in the fridge for about 30 minutes.

Cook the gnocchi, in batches, in boiling salted water for 4–5 minutes; when they are done they will puff up and rise to the top. Drain well, then quickly melt the butter, toss in the gnocchi and serve sprinkled with Parmesan cheese.

Spinach, Leek and Parmesan Risotto

Spinach is always a tricky one to get anywhere near children's mouths. So, as usual, good old risotto is a safe bet for slipping in those ingredients they always turn their noses up at. Spinach, for some reason, has always been unpopular with children, hence the Popeye connection. Children don't seem to know what you're talking about when you mention him now.

Serves 2 adults and 2 small children
Suitable for: 9 months + (omit seasoning for babies)

400g fresh spinach
2 leeks, finely shredded
1^1/$_2$ tablespoons olive oil
200g carnaroli or arborio rice
800ml vegetable stock
4 tablespoons double cream
60g Parmesan cheese, freshly grated

Wash the spinach, remove any stalks, then blanch in boiling, lightly salted water for 2 minutes, until tender. Drain very thoroughly and chop finely.

Gently cook the leeks in the olive oil until soft. Add the rice and stir over a low heat for a minute or so until it turns translucent. Heat the stock to simmering point in a separate pan. Gradually add the hot stock to the rice, a ladleful at a time, stirring constantly and ensuring that it has been fully absorbed by the rice before adding the next batch. After about 20–25 minutes, when the rice is just done (there may be some stock left), stir in the cooked spinach and the cream. Cook for 5 minutes, then stir in the Parmesan. Season to taste and serve.

Spring Herb Risotto with Courgettes

Courgettes work well with the herbs and Parmesan. You can vary the type you use, depending on what's available; yellow, white and round courgettes can be found in specialist shops and large supermarkets these days.

Serves 2 adults and 2 small children
Suitable for: 9 months + (omit seasoning for babies)

800ml vegetable stock
3 small courgettes, cut into 1cm dice
1 tablespoon olive oil
200g carnaroli or arborio rice
3 tablespoons finely chopped mixed chervil, parsley and chives
4 tablespoons double cream
30g Parmesan cheese, freshly grated

Bring the vegetable stock to the boil, add the courgettes and simmer for 3–4 minutes, until just tender. Remove the courgettes with a slotted spoon and set aside. Keep the stock hot.

Heat the olive oil in a heavy-based pan, add the rice and stir over a low heat for a minute or so until it turns translucent. Gradually add the hot stock, a ladleful at a time, stirring constantly and ensuring that it has been fully absorbed by the rice before adding the next batch. After about 20–25 minutes, when the rice is almost cooked, add the courgettes and herbs. Keep adding the stock in the same way as before until the rice is just cooked: the risotto should be quite moist. Stir in the cream and Parmesan, season to taste and serve.

Meat and Fish

117 Granny's Home-cooked Ham
117 Lamb's Liver with Bacon, Mash
     and Savoy Cabbage
119 Bangers and Mash with Onion Gravy
119 Toad in the Hole
121 Shepherd's Pie
123 Little Chicken and Ham Pies
125 Roast Poussin with Bread Sauce
127 Coronation Chicken
127 Parmesan-fried Chicken Escalopes
129 Fergus Henderson's Crispy Pig's Tails
131 Hamburgers
131 Paul Heathcote's Lancashire Hot-pot
135 Smoked Haddock with Poached Egg
     and Colcannon
135 Cod Fillet with Parsley Sauce and Mash
137 Real Fish Fingers
137 Salmon Casserole with Petits Pois
139 Kedgeree
139 Fishcakes with Herb Sauce
141 Tuna Burgers
141 Tuna Bolognese Sauce
143 Fish Pie with Fennel

In my experience, small children are carnivores. They love gnawing on bones or crunching the crisp skin of a roast, and pork crackling is always a treat. This instinctive pleasure in the nuts and bolts of meat is often forgotten as they grow older, along with those cuts that provide the meatiest mouthful.

London chef Fergus Henderson and his young family happily sit down to a snack of breaded pig's tails (see recipe on page 129). They might not seem an obvious choice but it's the same principle as pork scratchings, and they go down surprisingly well with some children. Not everyone feels up to cooking pig's tails but there are plenty of other flavoursome, good-value cuts to try, such as shanks, flank and shin, not to mention offal and rabbit. These are all coming back into fashion in restaurants and are easy to cook at home as well. It's rather sad that chicken breast is many people's favourite cut of meat, since it's one of the blandest. That said, it does take up flavours well and is ideal for Coronation Chicken salad (see page 127).

I love roasting meat; it's easy and delicious. Many parents roast a chicken every week because they know their children will eat it, inadvertently consuming the odd carrot or even some greens at the same time. A roast is also a great way to simplify the following night's supper. Try making leftovers into a curry, a risotto, little pastry pies or a traditional cottage pie. Boiling or baking your own ham (see page 117) may seem old-fashioned but it is no hassle and children will love the sandwiches.

My experience both in restaurants and at home shows that there's nothing like soft potato and fish or meat to tempt the fussiest eater – this is comfort food at its best. Unfortunately, disguising fish for children has become the norm. I blame this on fish fingers. Most commercial ones are low in fish but they become a habit for all concerned. Children love the taste, they're quick to prepare, and you can con yourself that your children are eating something vaguely healthy. Making proper fish fingers with fresh breadcrumbs (see page 137) will give them the opportunity to taste the real thing. What's more, goujons, as they are properly known, are a lot more appealing for grown-ups.

My friend and fellow restaurateur Tony Allan has two kids, Hollie and Charley, and their favourite dish is Tuna Burgers (see page 141), a perfect example of fish in drag. Add coriander, fresh salad leaves and a light chilli dressing or a squeeze of lime to make a delicious light meal for all ages. If you make smaller patties for children you will find they eat a lot more. Similarly, fishcakes can be tiny snacks to pop into your mouth or large enough for a satisfying meal. Try substituting different types of fish for a simple, unobtrusive way to introduce new flavours.

Granny's Home-cooked Ham

I often think back to my childhood and the smell of my grandmother Ellen's pot of ham knuckles or hocks simmering away on the back of the stove for 2–3 hours. She used to pay almost nothing for them in the Co-op but the flavour was infinitely better than any cooked ham you could buy. And the best thing was that she used to stick them in a pot of water, nothing else, and forget about them.

It's a shame that more people don't make the effort (no effort involved actually, just a bit of simmering) to do the same thing now. Perhaps vinyl slices of prepacked ham would then lose their appeal.

I'm not sure that the simplicity of cooking a bit of ham warrants a recipe. The only thing to remember is that it needs about 12 hours' soaking in cold water before cooking. Then drain it, put it in a large pan of cold water and bring slowly to the boil, skimming off any scum that forms on the top. Cook for 25 minutes per 500g, plus 25 minutes, timing the cooking from when the water comes to the boil. But the fun thing to do is drop some whole carrots, leeks, onions and celery into the pot about an hour before the end of the cooking time and eat them with the sliced ham. My gran never did that.

Lamb's Liver with Bacon, Mash and Savoy Cabbage

I love liver and can never understand why it is so unpopular with adults, let alone with children. It's full of flavour as well as being one of the best sources of iron. The problem seems to be more about texture and this is probably because most people only ever eat liver that has been overcooked so much that it has become tough and tasteless. In fact, lamb's and calf's liver take only a minute or so to cook and should be firm and juicy, not dry.

Serves 2 adults and 2 small children
Suitable for: 1 year +

200g Savoy cabbage, cut into rough dice
100g streaky bacon, rind removed
1 tablespoon vegetable oil
200g lamb's liver (any sinew removed), thinly sliced
1 quantity of Proper Mashed Potato (see page 75)
A knob of butter (optional)

Cook the cabbage in boiling salted water for 5 minutes and then drain in a colander. Lightly grill the bacon and cut into bite-sized pieces. Meanwhile, heat the oil in a large, heavy-based frying pan, add the liver and fry for 1 minute per side or until nicely coloured. Cut it into pieces like the bacon. Mix together the cabbage, bacon, liver and potato and reheat briefly in the frying pan. Stir a knob of butter through it if you wish, plus some salt and pepper, then serve.

Bangers and Mash with Onion Gravy

If you are going to feed sausages to children, make sure you give them proper ones, with a high meat content and natural ingredients. Cheap, poor-quality sausages contain the worst assortment of artificial ingredients and bear no relation to the real thing in terms of flavour. If you are lucky enough to have a sausage shop close to you, or a butcher's that sells sausages made on the premises, then you can buy little chipolatas. Some of the flavoured ones may taste too strong for your children and put them off, so until they get used to the natural flavour of good sausagemeat, keep it simple. Natural sausage skins can be a bit tougher, so you may need to remove them after cooking.

Serves 2 adults and 2 small children
Suitable for: 1 year +

10–12 good-quality sausages
1 quantity of Proper Mashed Potato (see page 75)

For the onion gravy:
2 onions, peeled and thinly sliced
Leaves from a sprig of thyme, chopped
1 tablespoon vegetable oil
10g butter
1 teaspoon tomato purée
20g plain flour
300ml chicken stock

For the gravy, gently cook the onions and thyme in the oil until soft, then add the butter, turn up the heat and cook for a few minutes more to colour the onions. Add the tomato purée and flour and stir well, then gradually add the chicken stock, stirring constantly. Bring to the boil and simmer for 25–30 minutes; the gravy should be quite thick and have a nice shine. Season to taste. Grill the sausages and serve on the mashed potato with the onion gravy.

Toad in the Hole

Toad in the Hole is one of those comfort foods that we often forget about. It makes a delicious supper and children are usually amused by the name.

Serves 2 adults and 2 small children
Suitable for: 1 year +

3 eggs
160g plain flour
300ml milk
6 good-quality chipolatas
6 tablespoons vegetable oil
1 quantity of Onion Gravy (see left)

Whisk the eggs in a bowl, then add half the flour and a little milk. Mix well, then add the rest of the flour and some salt and pepper. Gradually whisk in the rest of the milk to give a smooth batter. Leave to rest for half an hour. Meanwhile, lightly grill the sausages to colour them.

Divide the oil between 6 Yorkshire pudding tins and heat for a few minutes in an oven preheated to 200°C/Gas Mark 6. Cut the sausages in half, put 2 halves in each tin and fill with the batter. Return the tins to the oven and cook for 25–30 minutes, until crisp and well risen. Try to avoid opening the oven door as this may reduce the temperature and prevent the puddings rising. Serve with a generous helping of onion gravy.

Shepherd's Pie

Shepherd's pie is an ideal dish to feed to small children – soft in texture and rich in protein, carbohydrate, vitamins and minerals. Serve with Bashed Neeps (see page 91).

Serves 2 adults and 2 small children
Suitable for: 9 months +

1 small onion, peeled and finely chopped
1 small carrot, finely diced
1 clove of garlic, peeled and crushed
Leaves from a few sprigs of thyme, chopped
Leaves from a sprig of rosemary, chopped
1 tablespoon vegetable oil
400g finely minced lean lamb
15g plain flour
1 tablespoon tomato purée
A dash of Worcestershire sauce
400ml chicken stock
600g potatoes, peeled and cut into chunks
A knob of butter

Gently cook the onion, carrot, garlic, thyme and rosemary in the vegetable oil until soft. Add the minced lamb and cook on a high heat, stirring constantly, until it begins to colour. Add the flour, tomato purée and Worcestershire sauce, stir well, then gradually add the chicken stock. Bring to the boil, cover and simmer for about 45–50 minutes. If the mixture is looking a little dry, add some more stock or water. Season to taste, then transfer to 4 individual ovenproof dishes or one large one and leave to cool.

Boil the potatoes until tender, then drain well and mash with the butter and some salt and pepper. Pipe or fork the mashed potato on top of the lamb mixture and bake in an oven preheated to 200°C/Gas Mark 6 for 30–40 minutes, until lightly browned on top.

Little Chicken and Ham Pies

If you've recently cooked a chicken or a piece of ham or both, why not make some pies? Children like little individual ones because it feels as if they've been cooked specially for them, even if they are made from leftovers. I like to use non-stick muffin tins, as they give nicely shaped deep pies.

Makes about 12
Suitable for: 18 months +

350–400g good-quality puff pastry
40g butter
1 small onion, peeled and finely chopped
30g plain flour
200ml hot chicken stock
200–250g cooked and boned chicken, cut into small chunks
200–250g home-cooked ham (see page 117), cut into small chunks
1 tablespoon finely chopped parsley
1 egg, beaten

On a floured board or table, roll the puff pastry out to 2mm thick. Lay the pastry over the muffin tins and press it into the moulds. Carefully cut around the edges, leaving a bit of spare pastry to fold over the top of each pie. From the remaining pastry (re-roll the trimmings if necessary), cut out lids to fit the tins. Leave to rest in the fridge for 1 hour.

Meanwhile, melt the butter in a heavy-based pan and gently cook the onion without colouring, until soft. Add the flour and stir well, then gradually stir or whisk in the hot chicken stock. Bring to the boil and simmer on a low heat for 25–30 minutes, stirring occasionally, then season to taste with salt and pepper. Leave to cool, stirring occasionally to prevent a skin forming. The sauce should be thick.

Mix the chicken, ham and parsley together, then fold in some of the sauce until it just binds the meat (don't add too much or the pastry will go soggy). Fill the lined tins almost to the top with the mixture. Brush the edges of the pastry with some of the beaten egg and fold them over the pies. Place the pastry lids on top and press gently to seal. Brush with the remaining egg.

Cook the pies in an oven preheated to 200°C/Gas Mark 6 for 20–30 minutes, until golden brown.

Poussins are quick to cook and always taste juicy – unless you cremate them, of course. Unfortunately this often happens with poultry, from poussin to turkey, which is why people always comment that turkey is dry.

Poussins take just 15–20 minutes to cook in a hot oven or, if spatchcocked (ask your butcher to do this), even less time on a barbecue or under the grill. Mix some boned meat from the poussins with bread sauce to give babies a gourmet feed-up.

Serves 2 adults and 2 small children
Suitable for: 9 months +
(omit the seasoning for babies; bone and purée or very finely
  chop the chicken)

6 cloves of garlic, peeled
A few sprigs of thyme
3 oven-ready poussins
30g butter

For the bread sauce:
1 small onion, peeled and halved
30g butter
3 cloves
¹/₂ bay leaf
250ml milk
A pinch of grated nutmeg
50g fresh white breadcrumbs

For the bread sauce, finely chop half the onion and cook it gently in half of the butter until soft. Stud the other half of the onion with the cloves, pushing them through the bay leaf to anchor it to the onion. Put the milk, nutmeg and studded onion into the pan with the cooked onion and bring to the boil. Season with salt and pepper and simmer for 20 minutes. Remove the pan from the heat, cover and leave the sauce to infuse for 30 minutes or so.

Meanwhile, cook the poussins. Put the garlic and thyme into the stomach cavity of the birds and lightly season inside and out with salt and pepper. Rub the butter on the breasts and then roast for 15–20 minutes in an oven preheated to 230°C/Gas Mark 8. The best way to tell if the birds are cooked is to insert a roasting fork into the thickest part of a leg and lift it; the liquid that runs out should be clear.

Discard the studded onion from the bread sauce. Add the breadcrumbs to the milk and return the sauce to a low heat. Simmer for 10 minutes, giving it the occasional stir. Pour a third of the bread sauce from the pan into a blender and purée, then return it to the pan and stir in the remaining butter. Serve with the roast poussins.

Coronation Chicken

Unfortunately this dish has been badly made by many caterers and has now fallen out of fashion. It's a shame really because when it is prepared well it makes a perfect summer main course. A good introduction to curry flavours for young children, who enjoy the combination of mild spices and sweet mango chutney.

Serves 2 adults and 2 small children
Suitable for: 1 year +

3 chicken breasts, boned and skinned
Chicken stock to cover
$1/2$ small onion, peeled and finely chopped
1 clove of garlic, peeled and crushed
2 teaspoons very finely grated root ginger
1 tablespoon vegetable oil
$1^{1}/_{2}$ teaspoons ground cumin
$1^{1}/_{2}$ teaspoons curry powder
150g good-quality mayonnaise
A few sprigs of coriander, finely chopped
1 tablespoon mango chutney
A few leaves of Cos or Iceberg lettuce, shredded

Poach the chicken breasts in some chicken stock for 8–10 minutes, until cooked through, then leave to cool.

Gently cook the onion, garlic and ginger in the vegetable oil until soft. Add the cumin and curry powder and cook for 2–3 minutes, stirring occasionally. Add about 150ml of the stock that the chicken was cooked in and simmer for 10 minutes, until the liquid has completely evaporated. Leave to cool.

Mix the mayonnaise with the onion mixture, the coriander and the mango chutney (the chutney may need to be chopped finely if it is very chunky). Cut the chicken into 1–2cm cubes, or smaller for younger children, then mix with the mayonnaise. Season with salt and pepper if necessary. Serve on a bed of the shredded lettuce.

Parmesan-fried Chicken Escalopes

A dish that satisfies the breadcrumb fetish but with a little hint of Parmesan to make it slightly more sophisticated. Try to buy the fillet from the breast as it is very tender and a convenient size for children. Serve with Pasta Pomodoro (see page 101) to make a classic escalope milanaise.

Serves 2 adults and 2 small children
Suitable for: 1 year +

40–50g fresh white breadcrumbs
30g Parmesan cheese, freshly grated
8 pieces of chicken fillet
50g plain flour
1 free-range egg, beaten
Vegetable oil for frying

Mix the breadcrumbs with the Parmesan. Slightly flatten the chicken fillets between 2 sheets of clingfilm with a meat hammer or rolling pin, then season with salt and pepper, if you're using it. Lightly coat them in the flour, then the beaten egg and finally in the breadcrumb mixture. Heat some vegetable oil in a frying pan and fry the chicken fillets for 2–3 minutes on each side or until golden and cooked through.

Fergus Henderson's Crispy Pig's Tails

Fergus Henderson's restaurant is well-known for pioneering nose-to-tail eating. As mentioned in the introduction to this chapter, this is a dish that his family enjoys at home. Fergus reckons it appeals to the young gastronomic explorer thanks to the half-fat, half-flesh nature of a pig's tail plus a bone to gnaw on – it's not that children will eat anything in crispy breadcrumbs.

Serves 2 adults and 2 small children
Suitable for: 2 years +

4 long pig's tails
1 onion, peeled and roughly chopped
1 carrot, peeled and roughly chopped
1 stick of celery, chopped
A bundle of fresh herbs
1 bay leaf
5 black peppercorns
1/2 head of garlic
Grated zest of 1/2 lemon
600ml chicken stock or other light stock
1 tablespoon English mustard
2 eggs, beaten
Flour seasoned with salt and pepper, for dusting
100g fine white breadcrumbs
A large knob of butter

Place the tails in an ovenproof dish with the vegetables, herbs, peppercorns, garlic and lemon zest and cover with the stock. Cover the dish with foil, place in a medium oven preheated to 180°C/Gas Mark 4 and cook for 3 hours, checking occasionally that they don't cook too fast; when done you should easily be able to pinch through the flesh. Remove from the oven. Allow the tails to cool in the stock but remove them before it turns to jelly and drain any excess liquid off them (you can refrigerate them at this point).

When the pig's tails are cold and firm, mix together the mustard and eggs and have ready 3 bowls: flour, egg and mustard, and breadcrumbs. Dust the pig's tails with the flour, roll them in the egg and mustard mix, and finally coat them in the breadcrumbs so that they are well covered (do this just before you cook, otherwise the crumbs will go soggy).

Get a large ovenproof frying pan or a roasting tray hot, add the butter and, when it's sizzling, add the tails and roll them around (watch out, they can and will spit – be very careful). Place in a hot oven for 10 minutes, then turn them over, making sure there is enough butter, and roast for another 10 minutes, keeping an eye on them so they do not burn.

Serve hot. Some may like a spot of malt or red wine vinegar on their tails. Encourage the use of fingers and much gnawing of the bone.

Hamburgers

Fast food has given hamburgers a bad name but in fact they are a healthy and delicious meal for both adults and children as long as they are made with good-quality meat. If you prefer to avoid beef, try the tuna burgers on page 141.

Serves 2 adults and 2 small children
Suitable for: 18 months +

600g good-quality minced beef, including 20–30 per cent fat
160g tomato ketchup
40g American mustard
6 good-quality small baps
2 beef tomatoes, sliced
Dill pickles and slices of red onion, to serve (optional)

Mix the mince to ensure that the fat is evenly distributed throughout it, then season with salt and pepper. Mould it into 6 balls and shape it either with a burger press, if you have one, or simply by pressing it into a pastry cutter set on a board. Then put the hamburgers into the fridge to firm up before cooking. Whisk together the tomato ketchup and American mustard for the sauce.

Lightly toast the baps and keep them warm until you have cooked the burgers. They are best grilled on a barbecue or ridged grill pan but a smoking-hot cast-iron frying pan will do: this seals in the juices and will give a nicely cooked rare or medium-rare burger in a couple of minutes without the juices running out. Cook until well done for small children if you like. Don't cook the burgers under the grill unless you have a red-hot American-style one, as this tends to boil the meat so it becomes dry and flavourless.

Serve the hamburgers in the baps with the slices of beef tomato, plus dill pickles and red onion if you fancy, and the sauce.

Paul Heathcote's Lancashire Hot-pot

Paul Heathcote has two restaurants in his native Lancashire and one in Manchester. He is famed for his Lancashire Hot-pot, a peasant dish that, when cooked well, rivals any other. The ingredients provoke constant debate; potato, lamb and onion, the addition of carrot and stock or just cooked with water. Some recipes with an Irish influence even include oysters. When cooking for his children Paul occasionally tries to hide additional vegetables such as celery by cutting them very small; he substituted unsalted water for the stock when they were very young. Braised red cabbage is his favourite accompaniment; his children still prefer ketchup, which he hates to admit comes a close second for him too.

Serves 2 adults and 2 small children
Suitable for: 1 year +

6–8 middle neck lamb chops
675g potatoes, peeled and sliced
225g onions, peeled and sliced
300ml chicken or lamb stock
30g dripping (or butter), melted

Trim any excess fat from the chops and fry them on both sides in their own fat for a few minutes. Layer the potatoes, onions and chops in an ovenproof pot, seasoning between each layer and finishing with a layer of potatoes. Pour over the stock and brush the potatoes with the melted dripping.

Cover with a lid or foil and bake in an oven preheated to 190°C/Gas Mark 5 for 2–2¹/₂ hours. Remove the lid or foil, increase the heat to 230°C/Gas Mark 8 and allow the potatoes to brown for 20–30 minutes. Serve immediately, cutting the meat off the bones for small children.

Smoked Haddock with Poached Egg and Colcannon

Ask your fishmonger for natural smoked haddock as the yellow dyed version contains additives. If you can't find good smoked haddock, use fresh haddock instead and ask your fishmonger to skin it and remove all the bones.

Serves 2 adults and 2 small children
Suitable for: 1 year +

180–200g natural smoked haddock fillet
Milk to cover the haddock
1 quantity of Colcannon (see page 75)
4 free-range eggs

Double-check the haddock for bones, then poach it in milk for 5 minutes. Drain, leave to cool a little, then flake into the colcannon. Poach the eggs in an egg poacher and serve on top of the colcannon.

Cod Fillet with Parsley Sauce and Mash

This is a perfect family meal and a good way to get children to enjoy fish in its natural form. Cod was once considered to be a second-rate fish but depleted stocks of prime fish such as brill, turbot and sea bass meant that chefs began to think up more inventive ways to cook with cod. It now sits happily beside the best of fish on menus all over town.

Serves 2 adults and 2 small children
Suitable for: 9 months + (omit seasoning for babies)

4 x 90g cod fillets, skinned
25g unsalted butter
90ml milk
1 quantity of Proper Mashed Potato (see page 75)

For the parsley sauce:
300ml milk
$^{1}/_{2}$ teaspoon fennel seeds
2 small shallots, peeled and roughly chopped
45g unsalted butter
15g plain flour
3 tablespoons finely chopped parsley

First make the sauce: put the milk in a pan with the fennel seeds and shallots and simmer for 10 minutes. In a separate pan, melt 20g of the butter, add the flour and stir well. Gradually whisk in the milk, bring to the boil and simmer gently for 20 minutes. Strain through a fine sieve into a clean pan.

Carefully check the fish for bones, then put it in an ovenproof dish with the butter and milk. Cover with foil and bake for 10–15 minutes in an oven preheated to 180°C/Gas Mark 4. Meanwhile, stir the parsley into the sauce and simmer for 5 minutes. Cut the remaining butter into pieces and whisk into the sauce a few pieces at a time. Season with salt and pepper to taste.

When the fish is cooked, drain the milk off, add it to the sauce and put it back on to simmer for a few minutes. Serve the fish coated with the sauce and accompanied by the mashed potato.

Real Fish Fingers

A bit more labour intensive than reaching into the frozen foods compartment but worth it nutritionally. Limit preparation time by making a big batch of fish fingers and freezing them. Firmer fish holds together better and makes more evenly shaped fingers.

Serves 2 adults and 2 small children
Suitable for: 9 months + (omit seasoning for babies)

250g fresh firm white fish fillet, such as cod, halibut
  or haddock, skinned
60g plain flour
1 free-range egg, beaten
100g fresh white breadcrumbs
Vegetable oil for frying

Carefully check the fish for bones, then cut it into fingers approximately 6 x 2cm and season with salt and pepper. Spread the flour in one shallow dish, put the beaten egg in another and the breadcrumbs in a third. Coat the pieces of fish first in the flour, then the egg and finally the breadcrumbs.

Heat some vegetable oil in a heavy-based frying pan and cook the fish fingers for about 2–3 minutes on each side, until nicely browned. Drain on kitchen paper, then serve.

Salmon Casserole with Petits Pois

This is quite a colourful little casserole, pink, white and green. Serve it in a glass or transparent plastic bowl with Proper Mashed Potato (see page 75).

Serves 2 adults and 2 small children
Suitable for: 9 months + (omit seasoning for babies)

300g salmon fillet, skinned and diced
200ml milk
30g butter
20g plain flour
90g frozen petits pois or shelled fresh peas
1 teaspoon sugar (optional)
4 tablespoons double cream
A sprig of mint, finely chopped

Poach the salmon in the milk for 3–4 minutes, then spoon out on to kitchen paper. Melt the butter in a separate pan, stir in the flour and cook on a low heat for a minute, then gradually whisk in the milk the salmon was cooked in. Simmer gently for 30 minutes and then strain through a fine sieve into a clean pan. Meanwhile, if using fresh peas, cook them in boiling salted water with the sugar for about 10 minutes or until tender, then drain.

Add the fresh or frozen peas to the sauce with the cream and mint and simmer for 5 minutes. Add the salmon, simmer for another 2–3 minutes, then season with salt and pepper to taste and serve.

Kedgeree

A good introduction to spices and, hopefully, to curry later on. Kedgeree is not really a hot dish – more fragrant, if you like.

Serves 2 adults and 2 small children
Suitable for: 1 year +

100g basmati rice
100g natural smoked haddock fillet, lightly poached
100g salmon fillet, lightly poached
1 egg, hard-boiled and chopped

For the sauce:
20g butter
1/2 small onion, peeled and finely chopped
1/2 clove of garlic, peeled and crushed
20g fresh ginger, peeled and finely grated
1/2 teaspoon ground turmeric
1/2 teaspoon ground cumin
1/2 teaspoon curry powder
5 fennel seeds
1/2 teaspoon tomato purée
100ml fish stock
100ml double cream

To make the sauce, melt the butter in a heavy-based pan and fry the onion, garlic and ginger without letting them brown. Add all the spices and fry for another minute to release the flavours. Stir in the tomato purée and fish stock and boil until reduced by half. Pour in the cream and simmer gently for 10 minutes. Purée the sauce in a blender, then pass it through a fine sieve.

Wash the rice three times in cold water and then cook it in plenty of lightly salted boiling water until just tender. Drain it and return it to the pan, off the heat, with a lid on (a little butter may be forked through it).

To serve the kedgeree, flake the poached fish, checking it for bones. Reheat the sauce and add the fish. Put the rice into a bowl, spoon over the fish and sauce, then scatter over the chopped hard-boiled egg.

Fishcakes with Herb Sauce

This recipe makes quite a lot of fishcakes but it's worth putting some in the freezer for later. Children seem to find them very appetising, probably because they remind them of big fish fingers.

Serves 2 adults and 2 small children
Suitable for: 9 months + (omit seasoning for babies)

450g white fish or salmon fillet, skinned
600ml milk
1 teaspoon fennel seeds
3 shallots, peeled and roughly chopped
40g unsalted butter
30g plain flour, plus extra for dusting
1 quantity of Proper Mashed Potato (see page 75), with no milk, butter or cream added
2 teaspoons tomato ketchup
1 teaspoon mustard (optional)
Vegetable oil for frying
A few sprigs of parsley and dill, finely chopped
4 tablespoons double cream (optional)

Double-check that no bones are left in the fish. Poach it in the milk for 3–4 minutes, then remove and drain on kitchen paper. Flake the fish. For the sauce, add the fennel seeds and shallots to the milk and simmer for 10 minutes. Melt the butter in a separate pan, add the flour and stir well, then slowly whisk in the hot milk. Bring back to the boil and simmer gently for 20 minutes. Strain the sauce through a fine sieve and put aside.

Mix the mashed potato, tomato ketchup, and mustard, if using, and season to taste, then mix in the poached fish. Shape the mixture into even-sized cakes with the help of a spatula or palette knife. Leave to rest in the fridge for 30–40 minutes.

Lightly flour the fishcakes. Heat some vegetable oil in a frying pan, add the fishcakes and fry for 2–3 minutes on each side, until golden brown. Put them in an oven preheated to 190°C/Gas Mark 5 for 10 minutes to finish cooking. Add the parsley and dill to the sauce, and the cream if you want, and reheat gently. Serve the fishcakes coated with the sauce.

Tuna Burgers

Tony Allan has a busy schedule running his wholesale fish business and ever-expanding restaurant empire. But he naturally wants his daughters, Hollie and Charley, not to grow up grabbing fast-food snacks (as Tony admits to doing himself). With Christian Delteil, his group head chef, he developed this tuna burger and Tuna Bolognese (see right), which he serves in his restaurant chain, FISH. Serve these burgers with some Pomodoro Sauce (see page 101) mixed with tomato ketchup to make a relish.

Serves 2 adults and 2 small children
Suitable for: 1 year +

300g fresh tuna, very finely chopped, then chilled
60g capers, rinsed and finely chopped
60g gherkins, rinsed and finely chopped
1 small onion, peeled and finely chopped
Vegetable oil for frying
4 small burger buns

Mix the tuna with the capers, gherkins and onion in a bowl and lightly season with salt and pepper. Mould into 4 burger shapes with a burger mould or simply by pressing the mixture into a pastry cutter set on a board, then refrigerate for 30 minutes to firm up the mixture.

Heat a little vegetable oil in a heavy-based frying pan and fry the tuna burgers for about 3 minutes on each side, keeping them a little moist in the centre (for adults and older children, cook for 1 minute only per side, to serve the tuna rare). Meanwhile, lightly toast the burger buns. Put the burgers in the buns and serve immediately.

Tuna Bolognese Sauce

This is a great idea that Tony Allan and Christian Delteil have come up with for their restaurant FISH. If you are wary about BSE, this recipe is both meat-free and very healthy.

I like this with potato gnocchi but it's also very good served with pasta.

Serves 2 adults and 2 small children
Suitable for: 9 months + (omit seasoning for babies)

1 tablespoon olive oil
300g fresh tuna, very finely chopped
Double quantity of Pomodoro Sauce (see page 101)

To serve:
1 quantity of Gnocchi (see page 105) or 200–250g pasta
Freshly grated Parmesan cheese (optional)

Heat the olive oil in a heavy-based frying pan and quickly fry the tuna for 1 minute, stirring it occasionally. Reheat the sauce if necessary, add the tuna and simmer for 5 minutes. Meanwhile, cook the gnocchi in a large pan of boiling salted water. Serve with the sauce poured over, and with Parmesan cheese if required.

Fish Pie with Fennel

Disguising fish in a tasty-looking pie is a good way of getting children to try it. This recipe contains three different type of fish but if, for example, your children don't like salmon, you could increase the quantity of the other fish. As always when cooking fish for children, check it carefully for bones.

If the fennel looks a little stringy, peel the outer stalks with a vegetable peeler.

Serves 2 adults and 2 small children
Suitable for: 9 months + (omit seasoning for babies)

1 small fennel bulb, finely diced
55g butter
20g plain flour
200ml vegetable or fish stock
150g white fish fillet, such as cod or haddock,
   skinned and diced
75g salmon fillet, skinned and diced
75g smoked cod or haddock fillet, skinned and diced
A few sprigs of parsley, finely chopped
3–4 medium potatoes, peeled and cut into chunks

Gently cook the fennel in 40g of the butter until soft, then stir in the flour and mix well. Gradually whisk or stir in the stock, bring to the boil and simmer gently for 15 minutes, giving it an occasional stir, until it has reduced and thickened slightly. Add the fish and parsley and simmer for 5 minutes, then season with salt and pepper to taste. Transfer the mixture to 4 individual ovenproof dishes or one large one and leave to cool a little.

Meanwhile, boil the potatoes until tender, then drain well and mash with the remaining butter and some seasoning.

Using a piping bag or a fork, cover the fish mixture with the mashed potato; you will find it easier if it's still warm. Bake in an oven preheated to 190°C/Gas Mark 5 for 15–20 minutes, until lightly browned on top.

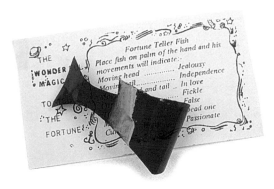

Puddings

149 Chocolate Chip Cookies

151 Creamy Sweet Polenta with Mango
and Mascarpone

151 Sophie's Apricot and Vanilla Compote

153 Sweet Couscous with Raisins and Yoghurt

153 Rhubarb Cream

155 Simple Little Chocolate Pots

155 Henry Harris's Meringues, Cranberries
and Ice Cream

157 Pancakes

157 Raspberry and Peach Crumble

159 Elderflower Jelly with Summer Fruits

159 Jam Roly Poly

161 Pain Perdu with Roasted Banana

161 Blueberry Muffins

163 Summer Fruit and Amaretti Cake

165 Chocolate and Pineapple Sticks

165 Tropical Fruit Salad with Star Anise

167 Eton Mess with Strawberries

167 Jeremy Strode's Coconut Sorbet

Getting kids to eat pudding has never been a problem. Getting them to eat anything else is the difficult bit. So this chapter includes dishes that will appeal to children yet provide a fair degree of nourishment at the same time – Tropical Fruit Salad, Raspberry and Peach Crumble and Sweet Couscous with Raisins and Yoghurt, for example. However, there's no harm in indulging our children (and ourselves!) occasionally, so I've also included quite a few chocolatey options and the sort of gooey pudding that almost every child loves, such as Henry Harris's recipe for Meringues with Cranberries and Ice Cream (see page 155). These are meant to be occasional treats, not everyday fare. Most commercially prepared puddings contain enormous amounts of sugar and other additives, so you can be sure that home-made ones are a more wholesome alternative.

I wouldn't suggest making puddings for every meal – some slices of fresh fruit will usually suffice. Try to offer a good variety of fruit, though; most children understandably get bored with a choice of apple or banana. As well as soft fruits in season, such as peaches, apricots and berries, there are plenty of exotic fruits to choose from – mango, papaya, kiwi and even lychees can go down very well. Dipping fruit in chocolate (see page 165) is fun to do occasionally, especially for parties, and your children can help.

People tend to protest nowadays that they have no time for baking but there can be few better ways of passing a rainy Saturday afternoon with a small child than making some simple biscuits or cakes, and their sense of achievement afterwards will be immense. The recipes for Blueberry Muffins and Chocolate Chip Cookies (right) are very easy-going. Children can 'help' as much as they like and they'll still taste delicious.

Chocolate Chip Cookies

Cookies are quite simple to make and can be stored in an airtight container for up to a week. Kids really enjoy getting involved in the preparation of this recipe, particularly breaking off lumps of dough to make the cookies.

Suitable for: 18 months +
Makes 16–20

100g unsalted butter
60g soft light brown sugar
1 free-range egg, beaten
150g plain flour
1/2 teaspoon baking powder
A few drops of vanilla extract
100g good-quality dark or milk chocolate buttons

Cream the butter and sugar together by hand or in a food processor or mixer until light and fluffy. Slowly add the beaten egg, scraping down the sides of the bowl from time to time. Carefully fold in the flour, baking powder, vanilla extract and chocolate buttons. Leave the mixture to rest in the fridge for 30 minutes or so, until it is pliable but not solid.

Break off small lumps of the dough and place, spaced well apart, on a greased baking tray. Bake in an oven preheated to 180°C/Gas Mark 4 for about 8–10 minutes, until the cookies are light golden; they should still be a little soft to the touch. Transfer to a wire rack and leave to cool.

Creamy Sweet Polenta with Mango and Mascarpone

If you use very ripe mango you probably won't need to add any sugar or honey to the polenta.

Serves 2 adults and 2 small children
Suitable for: 8 months + (don't use honey for babies)

600ml milk
60g quick-cooking polenta
About 2 tablespoons brown sugar or clear honey
1 ripe mango, peeled and stoned
100g mascarpone cheese

Bring the milk to the boil in a heavy-based pan. Whisk in the polenta and cook over a low heat for 10–15 minutes, stirring with a wooden spoon. The polenta should be the consistency of a thick soup. Add the sugar or honey to taste and leave until the mixture is just warm.

Mash or finely chop the mango. Serve the warm polenta with a spoonful of mascarpone and the mango.

Sophie's Apricot and Vanilla Compote

Compote is very French and so is my friend Sophie. In France, when fruit is in abundance in season it is often made into a compote, to be eaten immediately or preserved in jars. Sophie likes to add a little orange flower water, which she says helps her children sleep. You can use this recipe for other fruit, such as peaches, apples, pears and plums. It's a great way of introducing fruit into the diet.

Serves 2 adults and 2 small children
Suitable for: 6 months + (purée the fruit for young babies)

500g fresh apricots, halved and stoned
2 tablespoons caster sugar
2 teaspoons orange flower water, or juice of 1/2 orange
1/2 vanilla pod, cut in half lengthways, or a few drops of vanilla extract

Put all the ingredients in a saucepan, add enough water to cover and bring to the boil. Simmer for about 15 minutes, until the liquid has evaporated and the apricots have broken down. You can cook it for less time if you prefer to keep the apricots intact.

Sweet Couscous with Raisins and Yoghurt

Couscous is perfect for young children as it is easy to eat and digest. This can be served as a pudding, a snack, or even breakfast. Any good-quality dried fruit could be substituted for the raisins, such as mango, figs, banana etc. Even if you buy the no-need-to-soak variety I would suggest that for this recipe they should be soaked for an hour or so.

Serves 2 adults and 2 small children
Suitable for: 9 months +

150g couscous
60g raisins, soaked in hot water for 20 minutes, then drained
250ml milk
$1/2$ teaspoon ground cinnamon
60g caster sugar
4 tablespoons plain yoghurt

Put the couscous and raisins in a bowl. Put the milk in a pan with the cinnamon and sugar, bring to the boil, then pour it over the couscous and raisins. Stir well and cover with clingfilm. Leave for 10 minutes, until the milk has been absorbed. Mix in the yoghurt – or just dollop it on top – and serve warm.

Rhubarb Cream

My childhood memories of rhubarb are of eating it stewed or as jam. Cream was never an option. This creamy pink mixture is far more appealing and should please those little eyes and palates.

Serves 2 adults and 2 small children
Suitable for: 1 year +

200g rhubarb, cut into 2cm lengths
4 tablespoons water
155g caster sugar
90ml apple juice
Juice of $1/4$ lemon
250ml double cream

Put the rhubarb in a pan with the water and 30g of the sugar. Cook on a low heat for 10 minutes or until it has a jam-like consistency, then leave to cool.

Mix the remaining sugar with the apple and lemon juice. Add the cream and whip the mixture slowly with an electric whisk until stiff. Then fold three-quarters of the rhubarb into the cream mixture, put into individual glass dishes or a large serving dish and chill for 1–2 hours. Serve with the rest of the rhubarb on top.

Simple Little Chocolate Pots

All children love chocolate and these little individual pots are ideal for parties or even for taking on picnics.

Serves 4–6
Suitable for: 18 months +

300ml double cream
100g good-quality dark or milk chocolate, broken into pieces
1 tablespoon caster sugar

Bring half the double cream to the boil, add the chocolate and sugar, then remove from the heat and stir until the chocolate has dissolved. Leave to cool but don't let it set. Meanwhile, whip the rest of the cream until stiff.

Gently fold the melted chocolate mixture into the whipped cream until well mixed. Fill little cups or ramekins with the mixture and refrigerate for 1 hour or until set.

Henry Harris's Meringues, Cranberries and Ice Cream

Henry Harris is chef at Harvey Nichols' Fifth Floor restaurant. His children, Georgia and Noah, adore meringues and think that no birthday is complete without them. They have a very clear idea of what constitutes a proper meringue. It has to have a crisp, lightly coloured exterior and a chewy, gooey inside. There is only one way to achieve this and that is to make sure your oven is scrupulously clean. Any trace of grease or cleaning spray and the meringues will fall.

Suitable for: 2 years +
Serves 4–6

4 medium free-range egg whites
A pinch of salt
200g caster sugar
500g frozen cranberries
Juice and grated zest of 3 oranges
Juice and grated zest of 1 lemon
1/2 vanilla pod
400g demerara sugar
Good vanilla ice cream, to serve

Beat the egg whites and salt in a clean bowl until stiff. Add half the caster sugar and beat until stiff and glossy. Fold in the remaining caster sugar. Do this confidently so that the sugar dissolves into the meringue mixture. Place large spoonfuls on a baking sheet lined with silicone baking parchment and bake for 1 1/2 hours; the meringues should look and feel as described above.

Put the cranberries, orange and lemon juice and zest, vanilla pod and demerara sugar in a non-corrosive saucepan, bring to a gentle boil and then simmer slowly for about 40 minutes or until it forms a thick compote. Set aside to cool.

To serve, place a couple of meringues on each plate, top with some vanilla ice cream and then spoon over the compote. Retire to a safe distance as they tuck in!

Pancakes

Don't wait until Shrove Tuesday to serve pancakes. Kids can help make the batter and watch you try and perfect your toss. You can incorporate your favourite foods as sweet or savoury fillings – ham and cheese, mincemeat, banana, summer fruits. With pancakes you can use your imagination, but the classic lemon juice and sugar combination is hard to beat.

Serves 2 adults and 2 small children
Suitable for: 9 months +

120g plain flour, sifted
1 medium free-range egg
1 teaspoon caster sugar (for sweet fillings)
300ml milk
A little vegetable oil for frying

Whisk the flour, egg and sugar, if using, with one-third of the milk until smooth. Whisk in the remaining milk, then strain if necessary.

Heat a non-stick frying pan, rub with a little vegetable oil, then pour in a little of the batter. Tilt the pan immediately so that the mixture spreads evenly in a thin layer. After about 1 minute, when the pancake is lightly browned underneath, turn it with a spatula or palette knife – or toss it. Cook for another minute, until lightly coloured underneath, then turn out and serve. Make the rest of the pancakes in the same way.

If you need a large quantity of pancakes, you can make them in advance, stacking them up between squares of greaseproof paper, then reheat in the oven for a minute or so before serving. Alternatively the batter can be stored in the fridge for up to 2 days, then re-whisked before use – you may need to thin it with a little extra milk.

Raspberry and Peach Crumble

Fruit crumbles have interesting textures for children and you can make them any time of year using seasonal fruits such as apples, pears etc. Serve with thick custard, yoghurt or cream.

Serves 2 adults and 2 small children
Suitable for: 9 months +

4 ripe peaches, skinned and stoned
200g fresh or frozen raspberries

For the topping:
120g wholemeal flour
60g fine oatmeal
60g cold butter, cut into small pieces
60g light soft brown sugar

Cut the peaches into small pieces. Mix with the raspberries and put into 4 individual ovenproof dishes or one large one.

To make the topping, put the flour and oatmeal in a bowl and rub in the butter with your fingers until it becomes crumbly (this can be done in a food processor). Stir in the sugar, then sprinkle the crumble over the fruit. Bake in an oven preheated to 190°C/Gas Mark 5 for 25–30 minutes, until the topping is golden. Leave to cool a little before serving.

Elderflower Jelly with Summer Fruits

All children love jelly and, although this one looks sophisticated, it is very simple to make. You can vary the fruit depending on the time of year but the jelly won't set if you use acidic fruit like pineapple because the acid breaks down the gelatine. Depending on the moulds you use, you can make individual jellies or one great big one. Serve it to adults as a dinner-party dessert with some fruit purée and crème fraîche on the side.

Serves 4–6
Suitable for: 1 year +

800ml water
Juice of 1 lemon
400g caster sugar
40g leaf gelatine
100ml elderflower cordial
200g mixed berries (strawberries, raspberries, blueberries, blackberries etc)

Bring the water and lemon juice to the boil, add the sugar and stir until dissolved, then remove from the heat. Soak the gelatine leaves in cold water for a minute or so until soft. Gently squeeze out the water, add the gelatine to the sugar syrup and stir until dissolved. Add the elderflower cordial, then leave the jelly to cool but do not let it set.

Put the berries in a 1.5 litre jelly mould or 4–6 individual moulds, then pour in the jelly. Put in the fridge for an hour or so to set.

Jam Roly Poly

Even the name of this good old-fashioned pudding is tempting. And if your children don't like it I'm sure you'll be able to finish theirs up. Serve with cream or thick custard.

Serves 2 adults and 2 small children
Suitable for: 18 months +

100g plain flour
100g strong flour
1 tablespoon baking powder
A pinch of salt
50g light brown sugar
115g suet
Grated zest of 1/2 lemon
About 150ml water
5 tablespoons strawberry or blackcurrant jam, warmed
Milk for brushing
Demerara or granulated sugar for sprinkling

Sift the flours, baking powder and salt into a bowl, then stir in the sugar, suet and lemon zest. Add enough water to bind to a soft but not sticky dough. Roll out on a floured surface to a rectangle about 5mm thick, then spread with the warmed jam, leaving a 1cm border. Roll up loosely and join the ends together to seal. Place on a greased baking tray, brush with milk, then sprinkle with sugar. Bake in an oven preheated to 200°C/Gas Mark 6 for 30–40 minutes, until golden brown.

Pain Perdu with Roasted Banana

A simple, classic French dish of sweet fried bread. Eat it for breakfast, lunch or dinner, and try different toppings such as pears or berries.

Serves 2 adults and 2 small children
Suitable for: 1 year +

4 slices of bread cut 2cm thick, crusts removed
2 free-range eggs, beaten
1 tablespoon caster sugar, mixed with 1 teaspoon
  ground cinnamon
60g butter
Crème fraîche, fromage frais or ice cream, to serve

For the roasted bananas:
60g butter
4 large bananas, peeled and cut in half
2 tablespoons caster sugar

For the bananas, heat the butter in a frying pan that will go into the oven. When it is foaming, add the bananas and sugar, stir well, then transfer to an oven preheated to 220°C/Gas Mark 7. Roast for 10–15 minutes, until golden, giving the occasional stir. Meanwhile, dip the bread in the beaten egg, then dust with the caster sugar and cinnamon mixture. Heat the butter in a large frying pan and cook the bread for about a minute on each side, until crisp and golden.

To serve, cool the bananas a little and put two halves on top of each piece of toast. Serve with crème fraîche, fromage frais or ice cream.

Blueberry Muffins

Frozen blueberries are best here because the juices turn the mix an interesting colour. You can vary the basic muffin recipe by replacing the blueberries with chocolate drops or with chopped dried fruits such as apricots, soaked in hot water for an hour.

Makes 12–14
Suitable for: 1 year+

220g unsalted butter
110g caster sugar
$1^1/_2$ tablespoons honey
3 medium free-range eggs, beaten
260g plain flour
4 teaspoons baking powder
150ml milk
250g fresh or frozen blueberries

Using an electric mixer, cream the butter, sugar and honey together until light and fluffy. Turn the speed down and gradually beat in the eggs. Sift the flour and baking powder together, then carefully fold into the mixture. Mix in the milk, then the blueberries – if using frozen ones, stir well until the mixture begins to turn blue.

Spoon the mixture into greased deep muffin tins and bake for 15–20 minutes in an oven preheated to 180 °C/Gas Mark 4. Test by pressing the top of a muffin with your finger; it should be springy. Turn out on to a wire rack and leave to cool.

Summer Fruit and Amaretti Cake

This quick and simple cake is rather like a millefeuille. Children like it because of the colourful fruit layers and because it's deliciously messy to eat. Filo is easy to use and the components of the cake can be prepared the day before and assembled at the last minute. If you use alternative fruits, make sure you choose different colours.

Serves 4–6
Suitable for: 18 months +

50g unsalted butter
50g icing sugar
16 sheets of filo pastry
300ml double cream
100g caster sugar
150g fresh or frozen raspberries
150g fresh or frozen blueberries
1 mango, peeled and stoned
200g amaretti biscuits, coarsely crushed

Be careful when using filo pastry; it doesn't contain any fat so it dries up in no time. Always keep the pastry you are not working with covered with a lightly dampened tea towel.

Melt the butter and icing sugar together. Trim the filo sheets so they are about 20cm square. Lay a sheet of filo on a work surface and lightly brush with the butter mixture. Brush another sheet and lay it on top, then repeat with 2 more sheets. Repeat this 3 times with the remaining filo, so you have 4 stacks of 4 sheets. Place on baking sheets and bake in an oven preheated to 190°C/Gas Mark 5 for 5–10 minutes or until golden. Transfer to a wire rack to cool.

Whisk the cream and caster sugar together until stiff (but not overwhipped) and then divide between 3 bowls. Mash the fruits separately and mix each one into a bowl of cream. If the cream goes runny, just carefully whip it up again; the juice in the fruit will have diluted it.

To assemble the cake, spread one of the fruit and cream mixtures over one filo stack, then build up the cake with the other 2 creams and the remaining 3 stacks of filo (leave a couple of spoonfuls of cream to go on the very top layer to stick on the amaretti biscuits).

Once the layers are complete, smooth the sides with a palette knife or spatula, spread the extra spoonfuls of cream mixture on top, then scatter the amaretti biscuits on top and press them on to the sides.

Chocolate and Pineapple Sticks

A great party snack, this satisfies the chocolate craving and provides vitamins from the fruit at the same time. Other fruit can be used, such as melon, strawberries and mango. Another good way to serve it is to freeze the fruit on the sticks for an hour, then let the children dip the fruit in the chocolate themselves. This can be messy, as you can imagine, so you might prefer to stick to the first option.

You will need sixteen 16cm bamboo skewers. For very young children, remove the sticks before serving.

Suitable for: 18 months +

1 small ripe pineapple, peeled and cored
200–250g good-quality dark or milk chocolate, broken into small pieces

Cut the pineapple into small chunks and dry on kitchen paper. Skewer about 4 pieces on each stick. If serving immediately, put on a tray and place in the freezer for about an hour; or refrigerate and freeze later.

Melt the chocolate in a bowl set over a pan of simmering water, making sure the water isn't touching the base of the bowl. Dip the pineapple sticks into the chocolate until coated, then lay them on a tray lined with clingfilm. Refrigerate for 30 minutes before serving.

Tropical Fruit Salad with Star Anise

A refreshing summer or winter fruit salad with a hint of aniseed. You can vary the fruit according to what's in season and your own taste.

Serves 2 adults and 2 small children
Suitable for: 9 months +

1/2 pineapple, peeled, cored and cut into small cubes
2 bananas, peeled and sliced
1 mango, peeled, stoned and cut into small cubes

For the syrup:
2 star anise
60g caster sugar
50ml orange juice
50ml water

Put all the ingredients for the syrup in a small pan, bring to the boil and simmer for 2–3 minutes. Leave to cool.

Remove the star anise from the syrup. Pour the syrup over the fruit and chill for 1 hour before serving.

Eton Mess with Strawberries

A simple, creamy dessert that you can make with almost any soft fruits. The meringue is the most time-consuming part, so make it one or two days in advance, or cheat and buy some good-quality meringues.

An indulgent way to make this into a really luxurious dish is to use wild strawberries – not something regularly found at your local greengrocer's but it is possible to grow them at home. Just buy some plants from a good garden centre. The children will have fun picking these miniature delights.

Serves 2 adults and 2 small children
Suitable for: 18 months +

250ml double cream
60g caster sugar
A few drops of vanilla extract
200g strawberries

For the meringue:
2 free-range egg whites
120g caster sugar

To make the meringue, whisk the egg whites until stiff, then gradually whisk in half the caster sugar until the mixture forms stiff peaks. Fold in the remaining sugar. Spread the meringue on a baking tray lined with silicone baking parchment and place in the oven at the lowest temperature setting. Leave for about 2 hours or until dry and brittle.

Break the meringue into small pieces. Whip the double cream with the sugar and vanilla extract until stiff. Purée half the strawberries in a blender and slice the remaining ones into quarters. Fold the meringue and strawberry purée into the cream with half the sliced strawberries. Serve in small bowls with the rest of the strawberries scattered on top.

Jeremy Strode's Coconut Sorbet

Jeremy serves this in his Melbourne restaurant, Pomme, with a lime soufflé. But his son, Max, likes the sorbet best on its own. This recipe makes a lot but it's bound to get eaten up quickly. If making it for adults only, you could add 3 tablespoons of rum with the sugar syrup.

Serves 8
Suitable for: 1 year +

750ml milk
1/2 vanilla pod, or a few drops of vanilla extract
500g desiccated coconut
275g caster sugar
275ml water
500ml coconut cream
400ml double cream

Put the milk and vanilla in a saucepan and bring to the boil. Put the desiccated coconut in a bowl, pour the hot milk over, then cover and leave to infuse for 3 hours. Pass through a sieve, squeezing out all the liquid, and discard the desiccated coconut.

Put the sugar and water in a pan and bring to the boil, stirring to dissolve the sugar. Simmer for a few minutes to make a sugar syrup, then set aside. Put the coconut-flavoured milk, the coconut cream and the double cream in a separate pan and bring to the boil. Remove from the heat and stir in the sugar syrup, then leave to cool.

If you have an ice-cream machine, churn the mixture in this until set. Alternatively, pour it into a shallow container and freeze for an hour or so, until the mixture is slushy and beginning to set around the sides. Whisk until smooth (or whizz it in a food processor), to help get rid of ice crystals, then return it to the freezer. Repeat this 2 or 3 times and then freeze until firm. Transfer to the fridge about half an hour before serving.

Picnics, Snacks and Parties

175 Koftas with Minted Yoghurt
175 Courgette and Parmesan Sticks
177 Waffles
177 Tomato and Polenta Fingers
179 Scotch Quail's Eggs
179 Corn Fritters
181 Crudités with Guacamole
181 Houmous
183 Thai Summer Rolls
183 Sweet Potato and Parsnip Crisps
185 Chicken Satay with Peanut Sauce
187 Tortillas
187 Croque Enfant
189 Chocolate Toasties
189 Eggy Bread
191 Double Chocolate Rice Pyramid

When it comes to snacks, it's easy to forget all your good intentions and give in to junk food. But in fact snacks are an ideal opportunity to persuade children to be a bit more adventurous in their tastes. Most kids love dips, finger food and savoury toasts – all of which make ideal snacks – and will tolerate garlic, spices and other ingredients in them that they might not normally eat. Try Houmous (see page 181), Guacamole (page 181) and Croque Enfant (page 187) for quick but healthy fixes.

Children's parties can be the next most stressful thing after Christmas. Try to prepare as much of the food as possible in advance and, bearing in mind that children at a party will be too excited to grapple with anything more complicated than finger food, keep it simple. This doesn't mean that you can't produce a spread to dazzle the other parents (let's face it, it's not just the children who want to show off). The standard party menu of sausage rolls and Krispie cakes hasn't changed in years but a subtle variation on this theme can be far more visually impressive and much healthier. Try making your own sausage rolls with decent sausagemeat and ready-to-roll pastry – easy and delicious. Home-made Elderflower Jellies (see page 159) look stunning and can be made in a big batch. Sweet Potato and Parsnip Crisps (page 183) are naturally colourful and people will be amazed you have made them yourself. You needn't toil away alone. Your children will be far more excited about their party if they can help you prepare the food, lick the bowls, and decorate the biscuits and cakes etc.

Supermarkets and other shops have some great snack ideas these days. Mini pittas and tortillas make sandwiches more interesting. Stuff them with good-quality bought fillings or easy home-made ones (see Tortillas, page 187, for ideas).

Like most kids, my daughters were desperate to have a novelty cake for their birthday party. It looked great as they blew out the candles but as soon as they tasted it the novelty wore off, and most of it ended up in the bin. A birthday cake should make an impact but you don't have to be an expert with the piping bag. The Double Chocolate Rice Pyramid on page 191 is easy and fun to prepare. Spiked with sparklers, it has immense 'wow' factor and tastes great, too.

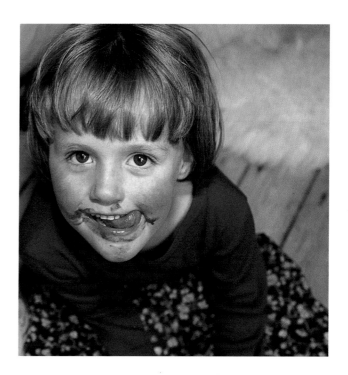

Koftas with Minted Yoghurt

An interesting little Middle Eastern snack. Food on sticks always appeals to kids but it's probably safer to remove the sticks for little ones. Serve with Couscous and Herb Salad (see page 83) and Houmous (see page 181) to make an infants' mezze.

You will need eight 14–15cm bamboo skewers, soaked in cold water for an hour.

Serves 2 adults and 2 small children
Suitable for: 1 year +

240g minced lamb
1 small onion, peeled and finely chopped
1 clove of garlic, peeled and crushed
A few sprigs of mint, finely chopped
A few sprigs of coriander, finely chopped
1/2 teaspoon ground cumin
A pinch of dried chilli flakes (optional)
A little vegetable oil

For the minted yoghurt:
3 tablespoons Greek yoghurt
A few sprigs of mint, finely chopped
1 teaspoon mint sauce
A pinch of ground turmeric

Mix all the ingredients for the minted yoghurt together and set aside.

Mix together the lamb, onion, garlic, herbs, cumin and chilli, if using, then roll into little sausage shapes (the size depends on the size of the mouths you are feeding) and mould on to the end of the skewers. Lightly rub with vegetable oil, cover the ends of the sticks with foil, and cook under a hot grill for 2–3 minutes or until browned all over, turning as necessary. Or cook on a barbecue. Serve with the minted yoghurt.

Courgette and Parmesan Sticks

I first saw these in a smart private Italian dining club, where the food is always inspiring and high quality. It serves them in matchstick-sized pieces which are difficult to replicate and keep crisp. So this is an equally delicious alternative for all. Especially the cook.

Serves 2 adults and 2 small children
Suitable for: 1 year +

4 medium courgettes
1 free-range egg
2 tablespoons milk
3 tablespoons plain flour
60g Parmesan cheese, freshly grated
Vegetable oil for deep-frying

Cut the courgettes into three, crossways, then cut each third into eight. Beat the egg with the milk. Have ready 4 dishes. Put the flour in the first, the beaten egg and milk in the second and the grated Parmesan in the third. The fourth is for the prepared courgettes. Coat the courgette pieces with the flour, then the egg and lastly the Parmesan. Make sure you shake off any excess flour before dipping them in the egg or the cheese will not stick.

Heat a deep-fat fryer to 160–170°C and cook the courgettes until golden. Drain on kitchen paper and leave to cool a little before serving.

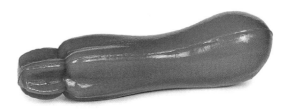

Waffles

Waffles are great fun, both at breakfast time and as a snack. The honeycombed texture just looks as if it was invented for children. I've given a recipe for a basic sweet waffle but if you want to make a savoury version, omit the sugar, replacing it with some grated Parmesan if you like. They can be bought ready-made, but that means missing out on lots of the fun.

You can use your imagination for toppings – anything from classic bacon and maple syrup to summer fruits with fromage frais.

Electric waffle machines are available in most good kitchen shops and are a good thing to have at the back of your cupboard. Or you may well have an old-fashioned cast-iron one tucked away somewhere.

Makes 6–8
Suitable for: 9 months +

130g plain flour
2 teaspoons baking powder
1 medium free-range egg, separated
250ml milk
40g butter, melted
A pinch of salt
1 tablespoon caster sugar
A little vegetable oil for greasing

Sift the flour and baking powder into a bowl. Mix the egg yolk, half the milk and the melted butter together and then mix with the flour and baking powder until smooth. Add the salt and sugar and gradually mix in the rest of the milk to form a smooth batter. Whisk the egg white until very stiff and fold into the batter.

Heat the waffle machine and rub lightly with oil. Pour in a little of the batter, but do not overfill as the mixture expands while cooking. Cooking time is normally about 2–3 minutes, but if you're new to waffle making it will take a few goes to get used to it. It's worth it, though. Serve immediately, or make a batch and reheat in a hot oven if necessary.

Tomato and Polenta Fingers

This contains plenty of tomato purée, which gives the fingers a good red colour. For adults, serve as a snack with drinks or as a starter with herb mayonnaise or tomato relish.

Serves 2 adults and 2 small children
Suitable for: 9 months + (omit seasoning for babies)

1 small onion, peeled and finely chopped
1 clove of garlic, peeled and crushed
Leaves from a few sprigs of thyme, chopped
2 tablespoons olive oil
40g tomato purée
200g tin of chopped tomatoes
250ml vegetable stock
60g quick-cooking polenta
30–60g Parmesan cheese, freshly grated
Vegetable oil for frying

Gently cook the onion, garlic and thyme in the olive oil until soft. Add the tomato purée, chopped tomatoes and vegetable stock and simmer for 10 minutes. Gradually stir in the polenta and simmer gently for another 10 minutes, stirring occasionally. Add the Parmesan and cook for 5 minutes, then season with salt and pepper if you wish. Spoon the mixture out into a square container in a layer about 1.5cm thick and leave to cool, then put in the fridge for 1–2 hours, until set.

Turn out the polenta on to a chopping board and cut into fingers. Heat some vegetable oil in a large, heavy-based frying pan and fry the fingers a few at a time until lightly browned. Drain on kitchen paper and serve.

Scotch Quail's Eggs

I used to make these for canapé parties years ago, then new ideas came along and the Scotch quail's eggs got left behind. Now I have found a new use for them. These miniature Scotch eggs are fun for children and adults, as a snack or starter. Be careful when you shell the eggs – they are delicate, as you can imagine. They are easiest to shell when just warm.

Makes 12
Suitable for: 1 year +

12 quail's eggs
350–400g good-quality sausagemeat
A few sprigs of parsley, finely chopped
Leaves from a few sprigs of thyme, finely chopped
Plain flour for dusting
1 large egg, beaten
150g fresh white breadcrumbs
Vegetable oil for deep-frying

Put the quail's eggs carefully into a small pan, cover with cold water, then bring to the boil and simmer for 3–4 minutes. Drain, run under cold water for a minute and then shell carefully. You will more than likely damage a few but don't worry – they can be patched up with sausagemeat. Wash them briefly in cold water to remove any shell.

Mix the sausagemeat with the herbs, then divide it into 12 little flat cakes. Flour your hands to prevent the mixture sticking to them, then mould it around the eggs. Place some flour, the beaten egg and the breadcrumbs in 3 separate dishes. Lightly flour each egg, dip it into the beaten egg, then the breadcrumbs and set aside. It's a messy job; they may need re-shaping in the palm of your hand.

Heat about 8cm of vegetable oil to 130°C in a deep-fat fryer. Cook the eggs for 3–4 minutes or until golden, then drain on kitchen paper. Serve hot or cold.

Corn Fritters

A tasty snack or accompaniment to a chicken main course. Spice up the mixture with a little finely chopped ginger, chilli and coriander. It makes a perfect pre-dinner drinks snack for adults.

Serves 2 adults and 2 small children
Suitable for: 1 year +

60g plain flour
1/2 teaspoon baking powder
A pinch of paprika
200g tin of sweetcorn, drained and roughly chopped
1 free-range egg, separated
50ml milk
Vegetable oil for frying

Sift the flour, baking powder and paprika into a bowl, then stir in the sweetcorn and egg yolk. Gradually add the milk to form a thick batter. Whisk the egg white until stiff, then fold in. Season with salt and pepper.

Heat a generous layer of oil in a large frying pan. Drop dessertspoonfuls of the mixture into the oil, flattening them slightly with the back of the spoon, and fry for about 2 minutes on each side, until crisp and golden. Drain on kitchen paper and keep warm while you fry the rest.

Crudités with Guacamole

Getting children to eat vegetables can be difficult but they generally seem to prefer them raw and crunchy. Vegetables for crudités should be colourful and completely fresh – the sight of a wizened old tomato can put children off completely. Get them to help arrange everything nicely on the plate, and perhaps offer other dips, too, such as Houmous (see right) and tomato salsa.

Serves 2 adults and 2 small children
Suitable for: 18 months +

10 asparagus tips or 100g green beans, or half quantities
  of each
1/2 cucumber
8 baby carrots or 3 medium-sized ones, peeled or scraped
90g yellow and red cherry tomatoes
8–10 baby sweetcorn
50g sugarsnaps or mangetout

For the guacamole:
1 ripe avocado
1 clove of garlic, peeled, blanched in water for 1 minute,
  then crushed
A pinch of cayenne pepper
2 tablespoons crème fraiche or soured cream
1 tablespoon chopped fresh coriander (optional)
Juice of 1/2 small lemon

Blanch the asparagus tips or green beans in lightly salted boiling water for 1 minute, then drain and refresh in cold water. Cut the cucumber into 8cm lengths, then slice into 8–10 wedges, cutting out the seeds. Cut the carrots into 8cm-long quarters if necessary. Arrange on a plate with the remaining vegetables.

For the guacamole, peel and stone the avocado and mash the flesh with a fork, or briefly in a food processor. Mix in the garlic, cayenne, cream and coriander, if using, then add the lemon juice to taste. Season with salt and pepper if you want. Serve with the crudités.

Houmous

Houmous makes perfect dipping food for children. Though lots of shops sell it ready-made, it often contains preservatives and other additives. Making your own is easy, particularly if you use tinned chickpeas.

Serves 2 adults and 2 small children
Suitable for: 9 months + (omit seasoning for babies)

400g tin of chickpeas, drained and rinsed
2–4 cloves of garlic, peeled and roughly chopped
Juice of 1 lemon
3 tablespoons extra virgin olive oil
3 tablespoons tahini
Flat bread or pitta bread, to serve

Put the chickpeas into a pan with the garlic and about 4 tablespoons of water. Cover and heat for 5 minutes, stirring occasionally. Remove from the heat and cool a little.

A good-quality blender produces the best houmous; otherwise use a food processor. Spoon the chickpeas and garlic into the blender or food processor with any remaining cooking liquid and blend on a high speed, stopping the machine occasionally to give the sides a scrape and stir the mix. When the chickpeas are fairly well blended, leave the machine running and gradually pour in the lemon juice, oil and tahini, again stopping the machine every so often to scrape down the sides. The houmous should be a thick pouring consistency while still warm. Season to taste with salt and pepper. Transfer to a bowl and leave, covered, at room temperature if serving that day, or refrigerate. Serve with warmed flat bread or pitta bread.

Thai Summer Rolls

These transparent rolls make delicious healthy snacks. The great advantage is that there's no cooking, so the flavours remain fresh and light. If you have an oriental supermarket close by, it shouldn't be a problem finding rice paper sheets but don't confuse them with the rice paper used for confectionery, which is not made of rice at all. Rice paper is a very natural product made from ground rice and water and dried on bamboo sheets. I used to walk past it in oriental shops without having a clue what it was.

You can use just vegetables or vegetables and meat as fillings; pork, chicken and duck work well. Serve with satay sauce (see page 185) or, for older children, a dip made of chilli sauce or other spicy oriental sauces.

Makes 8–12
Suitable for: 1 year +

2 spring onions, finely shredded
10–12 mangetout, finely shredded
2 large carrots, peeled and finely shredded
1 chicken breast, cooked and finely shredded
1–2 teaspoons sesame oil
1–2 teaspoons soy sauce
1 tablespoon chopped fresh coriander
8–12 small rice paper sheets

Mix together all the ingredients except the rice paper and season lightly with salt and pepper if necessary.

Take a shallow bowl large enough to hold the rice paper and half fill it with warm water. Put 2 or 3 pieces of rice paper at a time into the water to soften; this normally takes 2–3 minutes. Remove from the water and drain on kitchen paper. Put some of the chicken and vegetable mixture down the centre of each piece of rice paper and roll up as tightly as possible, then store, seam-side down, on a tray covered with clingfilm until required.

Sweet Potato and Parsnip Crisps

Vegetable crisps make excellent snacks and party food and look very impressive when you make them at home. They will keep in an airtight container for a few days so you can begin preparing your party in advance. Sweet potatoes and parsnips make good crisps as they have a naturally dry texture. But experiment with other vegetables, too, such as ordinary potatoes, beetroot or plantain.

The best way of slicing the vegetables is with a gadget called a mandolin. There are some very sharp Japanese mandolins on the market these days, so mind your fingers. You could also try a U-shaped, swivel-headed vegetable peeler or the large cutter on the side of a grater, although the results won't be as even.

Suitable for: 18 months +

2 orange-fleshed sweet potatoes
2–3 parsnips
Vegetable oil for deep-frying

The skin may be left on clean vegetables; otherwise peel them. Slice them as thinly as possible, keeping the potatoes and parsnips separate.

In a deep-fat fryer, heat about 10cm of vegetable oil to 170°C. Fry the slices in small batches, stirring occasionally. When they begin to colour lightly, after 1–2 minutes, remove them from the oil with a slotted spoon and drain on kitchen paper. They should crisp up as they cool down. If not, drop them back into the oil for a minute or so. You could season lightly with salt or use a mixture of celery and onion salt and paprika.

Chicken Satay with Peanut Sauce

Everyone's favourite oriental snack. Satay is good fun for parties but you have to make sure that the adults don't eat it all as soon as it appears. Because so many children seem to be allergic to nuts these days, you may want to make an alternative dip. Just substitute 50g cooked chickpeas for the peanuts.

This recipe has to be prepared a day in advance to give the chicken time to marinate. You will need twelve 12cm bamboo skewers, soaked in cold water for an hour.

Suitable for: 1 year + (remove the skewers for young children)

8 chicken breast fillets or 1 large chicken breast, skinned

For the marinade and sauce:
$1/2$ small onion, peeled and finely chopped
1 clove of garlic, peeled and crushed
20g root ginger, scraped and finely grated
1 teaspoon ground cumin
$1/2$ teaspoon ground turmeric
1 small chilli, seeded and finely chopped (optional)
3 tablespoons light sesame oil
1 teaspoon sugar
1 tablespoon Indonesian sweet soy sauce (*ketjap manis*) or
  light soy sauce
100ml chicken stock
50ml vegetable oil
50g roasted peanuts, washed

Gently cook the onion, garlic, ginger, cumin, turmeric and chilli, if using, in the sesame oil until the onion is soft. Add the sugar, soy sauce and chicken stock, bring to the boil and simmer for 10 minutes. Transfer to a food processor or blender, add the vegetable oil and process until smooth. Remove half for the marinade and put to one side, then process the rest with the peanuts to make the sauce.

If using chicken fillets, cut each one in half lengthways; otherwise cut the breast into 5mm strips. Thread the strips on to the skewers, then dip them into the marinade. Put into a container and pour the remaining marinade over the chicken. Cover with clingfilm and leave in the fridge to marinate for 24 hours, turning occasionally.

If you have a charcoal grill or ridged grill pan, then all the better. If not, remove any excess marinade from the chicken, lay the skewers on a grill pan and cover the exposed ends of the sticks with foil to prevent them burning. Cook under a hot grill for 3–4 minutes, turning them to cook evenly. If grilling over charcoal, ensure the ends of the skewers are not over the flame or direct heat. Stir up the sauce and serve with the chicken.

Tortillas

I recently cooked these for a grown-ups' casual dinner party. While filling the tortillas with guacamole, grilled vegetables and shredded chicken, I thought, surely this must be a perfect snack for children. They can get involved in making up their own filling and rolling the tortillas, then holding them in their hands to eat. After all, food needs to be fun.

Making your own tortillas is quite time-consuming but shopbought versions are now widely available and are generally very good quality; to be perfectly honest I use them a lot. Try to buy the thinnest tortilla possible. Just reheat briefly and then roll them up with the filling of your choice. Suggested fillings are given below but you can invent your own from the foods you are introducing to your child.

Suitable for: 9 months + (depending on the filling)

Suggested fillings:
- **Guacamole (see page 181)**
- **Simple grilled vegetables, such as courgettes, red peppers and aubergine**
- **Shredded grilled chicken breast, with shredded lettuce, soured cream and a spoonful of Pomodoro Sauce (see page 101) spiced up with a little chilli sauce**
- **Greek Salad (see page 85)**
- **Coronation Chicken (see page 127)**
- **Stir-fried vegetables**
- **Bacon, grated cheese, shredded lettuce and mayonnaise**

Croque Enfant

An infant version of the classic Croque Monsieur. You can vary the filling and even the type of bread you use. Sandwiches need not be boring sliced bread filled with cheese. If you are stuck for ideas, sandwich bars and supermarkets are good places to find inspiration for new fillings.

Serves 2 adults and 2 small children
Suitable for: 1 year +

8 thin slices of white bread
Unsalted butter for spreading
8 slices of good-quality ham
8 slices of Gruyère or Cheddar cheese

Butter the bread on both sides, then make 4 sandwiches with the ham and cheese (be generous) and cut off the crusts. Preheat the grill and toast the sandwiches for a couple of minutes on each side until golden.

Chocolate Toasties

I remember going to France on a school trip when I was at primary school and being given warm baguette and a chunk of chocolate. I think this recipe is a rewarding version for all palates.

Serves 2 adults and 2 small children
Suitable for: 18 months +

8 slices of good white bread or brioche
Unsalted butter for spreading
150–200g good-quality dark or milk chocolate, broken into
  small pieces

Butter the slices of bread on one side and then toast lightly on both sides. Make 4 sandwiches with the chocolate pieces, with the buttered side on the outside (don't put the chocolate too close to the edges of the bread or it will melt out). Toast the sandwiches until the chocolate begins to melt, then cut in half and serve immediately.

Eggy Bread

A classic French snack; add some slices of cheese or ham for a more substantial meal. This also makes a good breakfast or brunch with some grilled field mushrooms.

Serves 2 adults and 2 small children
Suitable for: 1 year +

6 thin slices of white bread, crusts removed
Vegetable oil for frying
2 free-range eggs, beaten

Cut each slice of bread into 4 triangles. Heat some vegetable oil in a heavy-based frying pan. Season the beaten egg with a little salt and pepper if you want, then dip the bread in it and fry for a minute or so on each side until golden. Drain on kitchen paper and serve.

Double Chocolate Rice Pyramid

Chocolate Rice Krispie cakes are a party favourite and kids love helping to make them. By accident whilst working on this book, we discovered that, rather like a classic French *croquembouche*, we could build a pyramid from chocolate Krispie cakes by dipping each one in a little more melted chocolate and stacking them up.

This has everything a child looks for in a cake: it's big, it's chocolatey and, with sparklers as candles, it makes a spectacular birthday statement. Unlike other cakes, where an adult has to get involved to do the cutting, the birthday boy or girl can break it up and give out the cakes by themselves. All this and it's actually quite healthy in comparison to the shopbought alternative because it only contains two simple ingredients.

When it comes to chocolate, quality is important. The higher the cocoa content, the less sugar, hydrogenated fat and artificial ingredients it will contain. Most children never get to taste good-quality plain chocolate because it is more expensive but, given the choice, they much prefer it. There are good-quality chocolate buttons or drops on the market now, which cut down on labour and melting.

Serves 10–12
Suitable for: 1 year +

300g good-quality white chocolate
500g good-quality dark or milk chocolate
240g Rice Krispies or other rice cereal

Melt the white chocolate and 300g dark or milk chocolate separately in 2 bowls set over pans of simmering water, making sure the water isn't touching the base of the bowls. Remove from the heat, then divide the Rice Krispies in half and stir into each bowl of chocolate.

Spoon the mixture into large paper cake cases and leave in a cool place to set for an hour or so.

Remove the paper cases. Melt the remaining dark or milk chocolate, then dip the cakes in it and stack them up to form a pyramid. The larger the cakes, the more stable the structure will be. You should let it set for a while half way through building or it is likely to collapse, as we discovered. Keep in a cool place until needed.

Drinks and Lollies

197 Lemonade

197 Pear and Ginger Juice

199 Strawberry and Banana Smoothie

199 Banana Smoothie

199 Banana and Peanut Butter Smoothie

199 Tropical Fruit Smoothie

201 Vanilla Milkshake

201 Banana Fromage Frais Milkshake

201 Lollipops

Don't be tempted by those handy little cartons of fruit juice. These products are not fresh but made from diluted concentrate and can be so high in natural sugars that they lead to tooth decay. Why not make fruit drinks at home instead? It's easy, you'll know exactly what goes into them, and you'll retain all the vitamins. Many people try to purée fruit in a food processor with poor results. A blender does a better job, particularly those powerful American bar blenders. If you want to make your own vegetable and fruit juices, a juice extractor is a useful piece of equipment.

Remember that for small children fruit juice should be an occasional treat and should always be diluted. It is better to give toddlers juice in a cup than a bottle as intermittent sucking leaves teeth and gums coated in sugar for much longer.

You needn't stop at plain juice. Combine fresh fruit with milk, yoghurt, fromage frais or even ice cream in the blender to make shakes, smoothies or simple baby and toddler puddings in seconds. Smoothies are easy to make and are a great combination of vitamins, minerals, protein and calcium. If you prepare the fruit in advance and store it in bags in the freezer your smoothies will have an ice-creamy texture. The recipes that follow are fairly flexible because you can make them thicker by adding more fruit or dilute them with extra liquid. Use any type of ripe, soft-fleshed fruit, such as berries, mango, papaya, banana, pear or a combination. Taste before serving to see if it needs any extra sugar but if the fruit is properly ripe it will probably be sweet enough.

Lemonade

Serves 6–8
Suitable for: 2 years +

Juice of 6 large lemons
60g caster sugar
1 litre sparkling mineral water

Bring the lemon juice and sugar to the boil, remove from the heat and leave to cool. Mix with the sparkling water and refrigerate.

Pear and Ginger Juice

Serves 2
Suitable for: 1 year +

6 ripe pears, peeled and cored
1 teaspoon finely grated fresh root ginger
100ml sparkling mineral water
A little sugar (optional)

Blend all the ingredients in a food processor, then strain through a fine sieve. Taste and sweeten with a little sugar if necessary. Chill for 1–2 hours.

Strawberry and Banana Smoothie

Serves 2
Suitable for: 1 year +

3 ripe bananas, peeled, chopped into small pieces and frozen
10 strawberries
300ml milk

Blend all the ingredients in a food processor until smooth. Serve in tall glasses with straws.

Banana Smoothie

Serves 2
Suitable for: 1 year +

3 ripe bananas, peeled, chopped into small pieces and frozen
300ml milk

Blend all the ingredients in a food processor until smooth. Serve in tall glasses with straws.

Banana and Peanut Butter Smoothie

Serves 2
Suitable for: 1 year +

3 ripe bananas, peeled, chopped into small pieces and frozen
1 dessertspoon smooth peanut butter
300ml milk

Blend all the ingredients in a food processor until smooth. Serve in tall glasses with straws.

Tropical Fruit Smoothie

Serves 2
Suitable for: 1 year +

1 banana, peeled
1/2 small pineapple, peeled and cored
1 papaya, peeled and deseeded
1 mango, peeled and stoned
250ml tin of coconut milk

Finely chop all the fruit and freeze. Blend all the ingredients in a food processor until smooth. Serve in tall glasses with straws.

Vanilla Milkshake

Serves 2–4
Suitable for: 1 year +

1 vanilla pod or ¹/₂ – 1 teaspoon vanilla extract, to taste
500ml milk
100g good-quality vanilla ice cream

If using a vanilla pod, cut it in half lengthways and scrape out the seeds. Put the vanilla seeds and pod, or the vanilla extract, into 100ml of the milk in a small saucepan. Bring to the boil and simmer gently for 3–4 minutes, then remove from the heat and leave to cool. Remove the vanilla pod, if using. Blend the vanilla-flavoured milk in a food processor with the rest of the milk and the ice cream, then serve immediately, in tall glasses with straws.

Banana Fromage Frais Milkshake

Serves 2
Suitable for: 1 year +

1 ripe banana, peeled
90–100g fromage frais
120ml milk

Chill all the ingredients, then blend in a food processor until smooth. Serve in tall glasses with straws.

Lollipops

Home-made lollipops used to be as synthetic as the shopbought version, because synthetic juices and cordials were used. Now delicious ices can be produced at home simply by puréeing fresh fruit and freezing it in ice-lolly kits or similar containers, or by freezing fresh juices. You can make some great combinations like mango and kiwi if you layer them: half-fill the containers with one juice or purée and freeze, then pour in the next and freeze until firm. Or make your own cocktails on sticks like summer fruits or melon and grenadine. Add something a little stronger for grown-ups, if you like.

Index

A is for Additives

Additives 49
Allan, Tony 115
Allergies 41, 47
Apple, *and Celeriac Mash* 89
Apricots, *Sophie's Vanilla Compote* 151
Aubergines, *Escalopes with Melted Mozzarella* 71
Avocados, *Crudités with Guacamole* 173, 181

B is for Babies

Babies 17, 37-51
Baby Rice 41, 49
Bacon
    Buttery Sugarsnaps 79
    Lamb's Liver with Mash and Savoy Cabbage 117
Baked Beans, *Home-made* 81
Bananas
    Fromage Frais Milkshake 201
    and Peanut Butter Smoothie 199
    Roasted with Pain Perdu 161
    Smoothie 199
    and Strawberry Smoothie 199
Basil, *Tim's Carrot Purée* 91
Biscuits, *Chocolate Chip Cookies* 149
Blueberries, *Muffins* 149, 161
Bolognese Sauce 141
Bread
    Eggy Bread 189
    Sauce 125
Broccoli, *Gratin with Mascarpone and Parmesan* 69, 81
Burgers
    Hamburgers 21, 131
    Tuna 115, 141
Butternut Squash Risotto 107

C is for Cookies

Cabbage, *Colcannon* 75, 135
Caesar Salad 27
Cakes
    Double Chocolate Rice Pyramid 173, 191
    Summer Fruit and Amaretti 163
Caribbean Vegetable Hotpot 73
Carrots
    and Cumin Soup 59
    Tim's Purée with Basil 91
Celeriac, *and Apple Mash* 89
Cheese
    Aubergine Escalopes with Melted Mozzarella 71
    Broccoli Gratin with Mascarpone and Parmesan 69, 81
    Courgette and Parmesan Sticks 175
    Creamy Sweet Polenta with Mango and Mascarpone 151
    Parmesan and Rosemary Baked Potato Wedges 77
    Parmesan-fried Chicken Escalopes 127
    Spinach, Leek and Parmesan Risotto 109
Chicken 115
    Coronation 115, 127
    Giant Pasta Shells with Herbs 105
    Little Chicken and Ham Pies 123
    Parmesan-fried Escalopes 127
    Roast Poussin with Bread Sauce 125
    Satay with Peanut Sauce 185
    Livers and Scrambled Eggs 101
    Stock 57
    and Sweetcorn Soup 61
    Vegetable and Lentil Broth 63
Chips 21, 77
Chocolate
    Chip Cookies 149
    and Pineapple Sticks 165
    Rice Pyramid 173, 191
    Simple Little Pots 155
    Toasties 189
Coconut, *Sorbet* 167
Cod, *Fillet with Parsley Sauce and Mash* 135
Coddled Eggs 21, 99

Colcannon 75, 135
Compote, *Sophie's Apricot and Vanilla* 151
Coriander, *Cumin-spiced Lentils* 79
Corn Fritters 179
Coronation Chicken 115, 127
Courgettes
   and Parmesan Sticks 175
   Spring Herb Risotto 109
Couscous
   and Herb Salad 83
   with Raisins and Yoghurt 153
Covent Garden 27
Cranberries, *Meringues and Ice Cream* 149, 155
Crisps, *Sweet Potato and Parsnip* 173, 183
Croque Enfant 173, 187
Crudités, *with Guacamole* 173, 181
Crumble, *Raspberry and Peach* 157
Cumin
   and Carrot Soup 59
   Lentils with Coriander 79
   Roasted Sweet Vegetables 69, 71

D is for Drinks
Drinks 41, 43, 195-201

E is for Eggs
Eggs 95-7
   Coddled 21, 99
   Eggy Bread 189
   Scotch Quail's Eggs 179
   Scrambled with Chicken Livers 101
   Smoked Haddock with Colcannon 135
   Spanish Tortilla 99
Elderflower Jelly, *with Summer Fruits* 159, 173
Equipment 51
Eton Mess, *with Strawberries* 167

F is for Fish
Farming 29
Fennel, *Fish Pie* 143
Fish 113-15, 135-43
   Cod Fillet with Parsley Sauce and Mash 135
   Fish Fingers 21, 115, 137
   Fish Pie with Fennel 143
   Fishcakes with Herb Sauce 139
   Kedgeree 139
   Penne with Tuna, Tomato and Olive Oil 103
   Salmon Casserole with Petit Pois 137
   Smoked Haddock with Poached Egg and Colcannon 135
   Tuna Bolognese Sauce 141
   Tuna Burgers 115, 141
   Tuna Pasta 97
Fromage Frais
   Banana Milkshake 201
   Iced Strawberry Soup 63
Frozen Food 51
   Purées 17, 41, 51
   Stock 55
Fruit
   Fruit Salad with Star Anise 165
   Juice 21, 197
   Puddings 149-67
   Purées 41
   Smoothies & Milkshakes 199, 201

G is for Gnocchi
Ginger
   and Pear Juice 197
   and Pumpkin Purée 87
Gnocchi 107
Gravy, *Onion* 119
Greek Salad 85
Guacamole, *Crudités* 173, 181

H is for Hamburgers

Haddock, *Smoked with Poached Egg and Colcannon* 135
Ham
    Home-cooked 115, 117
    Little Chicken and Ham Pies 123
Hamburgers 21, 131
Harris, Henry 149, 155
Heathcote, Paul 131
Henderson, Fergus 23, 115, 129
Herb Sauce 139
Houmous 173, 181
Hughes, Tim 91

I is for Ice Cream

Ice Cream, *Meringues and Cranberries* 149, 155

J is for Jam

Jam Roly Poly 159
Jelly, *Elderflower with Summer Fruits* 159, 173
Junk Food 19, 21

K is for Kedgeree

Kedgeree 139
Ketchup 47, 49
Koftas, *with Minted Yoghurt* 175

L is for Lollipops

Lactose Intolerance 47
Lamb
    Lamb's Liver with Bacon, Mash and Savoy Cabbage 117
    Lancashire Hot-pot 131
    Shepherd's Pie 121
Lancashire Hot-pot 131
Leeks 21
    Spinach and Parmesan Risotto 109
Lemonade 23, 197
Lentils
    Chicken and Vegetable Broth 63
    Cumin-spiced with Coriander 79
Lettuce, *Thousand Island Dressing* 69, 83
Locatelli, Giorgio 47, 49
Lollipops 201

M is for Meat

Mango, *Creamy Sweet Polenta with Mascarpone* 151
Mayonnaise, *Crushed Potato Mayonnaise* 85
Meat 113-31
    Bangers and Mash with Onion Gravy 119
    Buttery Sugarsnaps with Smoky Bacon 79
    Chicken Satay with Peanut Sauce 185
    Chicken Stock 57
    Chicken and Sweetcorn Soup 61
    Coronation Chicken 115, 127
    Crispy Pig's Tails 23, 115, 129
    Giant Pasta Shells with Chicken and Herbs 105
    Hamburgers 21, 131
    Home-cooked Ham 115, 117
    Lamb's Liver with Bacon, Mash and Savoy Cabbage 117
    Lancashire Hot-pot 131
    Little Chicken and Ham Pies 123
    Parmesan-fried Chicken Escalopes 127
    Roast Poussin with Bread Sauce 125
    Sausage Rolls 173
    Scrambled Eggs with Chicken Livers 101
    Shepherd's Pie 121
    Toad in the Hole 119
Meat, *Chicken, Vegetable and Lentil Broth* 63
Melon, *Soup* 63
Meringues, *Cranberries and Ice Cream* 149, 155
Microwaves 43
Milk 17, 41, 43, 47
Milkshakes
    Banana Fromage Frais Milkshake 201
    Vanilla 201
Mills, Laurie 33
Muffins, *Blueberry* 149, 161

N is for Neeps

Neeps, *Bashed* 91

O is for Organic

Onions, *Gravy* 119
Organic Food 29

P is for Parties

Pain Perdu, *with Roasted Banana* 161
Pancakes 157
Parsley Sauce 135
Parsnips
    Bashed Neeps 91
    and Sweet Potato Crisps 173, 183
Parties 171-91
Pasta 95-7
    e Fagioli 103
    Farfalle with Pesto 105
    Giant Shells with Chicken and Herbs 105
    Penne with Tuna, Tomato and Olive Oil 103
    Pomodoro 101
Peaches, *and Raspberry Crumble* 157
Peanuts
    Banana and Peanut Butter Smoothie 199
    Sauce 185
Pears, *and Ginger Juice* 197
Peas
    Purée 89
    Salmon Casserole with Petit Pois 137
    Soup 61
Pesto, *Farfalle* 105
Picnics 171-91
Pies
    Fish Pie with Fennel 143
    Little Chicken and Ham Pies 123
Pig's Tails, *Crispy* 23, 115, 129
Pineapples, *and Chocolate Sticks* 165
Polenta
    and Tomato Fingers 177
    with Mango and Mascarpone 151
Pomodoro Sauce 101
Potatoes
    Chips 21, 77
    Crushed Potato Mayonnaise 85
    Gnocchi 107
    Mashed 75, 117, 119, 135
    Parmesan and Rosemary Baked Potato Wedges 77
    Sweet Potato and Parsnip Crisps 173, 183
    Sweet Potato Rösti 69, 73
Presentation 17, 43

Puddings 147-67
Pumpkins, *and Ginger Purée* 87
Purées 17, 41, 43, 49
    Frozen 17, 41, 51
    Pea 89
    Roast Pumpkin and Ginger 87
    Tim's Carrot Purée with Basil 91
    Vegetable 41, 69, 87

Q is for Quails

Quail's Eggs 179

R is for Rhubarb

Raisins, *Sweet Couscous and Yoghurt* 153
Raspberries, *and Peach Crumble* 157
Restaurants 23
Rhubarb Cream 153
Rice 95-7
    Baby Rice 41, 49
    Butternut Squash Risotto 107
    Spinach, Leek and Parmesan Risotto 109
    Spring Herb Risotto with Courgettes 109
Rice Krispies, *Double Chocolate Pyramid* 173, 191
Roly Poly 159
Rosemary, *Parmesan and Baked Potato Wedges* 77
Rösti 69, 73

S is for Strawberries

Salads
    Caesar 27
    Couscous and Herb 83
    Crushed Potato Mayonnaise 85
    Greek 85
    Little Gems with Thousand Island Dressing 69, 83
Salmon, *Casserole with Petit Pois* 137
Salt 49
Satay, *with Peanut Sauce* 185
Sauces
    Bolognese 141
    Bread 125
    Herb 139
    Parsley 135
    Peanut 185
    Pomodoro 101

Sausages
    Bangers and Mash with Onion Gravy 119
    Rolls 173
    Toad in the Hole 119
Savoy Cabbage, *Lamb's Liver with Bacon and Mash* 117
Scotch Quail's Eggs 179
Shepherd's Pie 121
Shopping 21, 25-9
Smoothies 197
    Banana 199
    Banana and Peanut Butter 199
    Strawberry and Banana 199
    Tropical Fruit 199
Snacks 171-91
Sorbet, *Coconut* 167
Soups 53-63
    Carrot and Cumin 59
    Chicken and Sweetcorn 61
    Chicken, Vegetable and Lentil Broth 63
    Iced Strawberries with Fromage Frais 63
    Melon 63
    Minted Pea 61
    Tomato 59
Spinach, *Leek and Parmesan Risotto* 109
Star Anise, *with Tropical Fruit Salad* 165
Stocks 53-7
    Chicken 57
    Vegetable 57
Storage Times 51
Strawberries 27
    and Banana Smoothie 199
    with Eton Mess 167
    Iced Soup with Fromage Frais 63
Strode, Jeremy 167
Sugar 49
Sugarsnaps, *Buttery Sugarsnaps with Smoky Bacon* 79
Swedes, *Bashed Neeps* 91
Sweet Potatoes
    and Parsnip Crisps 173, 183
    Rösti 69, 73
Sweetcorn, *and Chicken Soup* 61

T is for Toddlers
Thai Summer Rolls 183
Thousand Island Dressing, *with Little Gems* 69, 83
Toad in the Hole 119
Toddlers 19, 37-51
Tomatoes
    Penne with Tuna and Olive Oil 103
    and Polenta Fingers 177
    Soup 59
Tortillas 99, 173, 187
Tuna
    Bolognese Sauce 141
    Burgers 115, 141
    Pasta 97
    Penne with Tomato and Olive Oil 103

V is for Vegetables
Vanilla
    Milkshake 201
    Sophie's Apricot Compote 151
Vegetables 67-91
    see also individual vegetables
    Purées 41, 69, 87
    Stock 57

W is for Weaning
Waffles 177
Weaning Times 39

Y is for Yum
Yoghurt
    Koftas 175
    Sweet Couscous with Raisins 153

The End